Medicine and Society in America

1660–1860

*

RICHARD HARRISON SHRYOCK

Cornell Paperbacks
Cornell University Press
ITHACA AND LONDON

CORNELL UNIVERSITY PRESS

First printing, Great Seal Books, 1962
First printing, Cornell Paperbacks, 1972

International Standard Book Number 0-8014-9093-6
Library of Congress Catalog Card Number 60-6417

PRINTED IN THE UNITED STATES OF AMERICA

Medicine and Society in America

1660–1860

In Memory of My Brother,

JOHN KNIGHT SHRYOCK

Preface

THE invitation received through Professor Bayrd Still to deliver the Anson G. Phelps Lectures in 1959 was doubly welcome. It offered, first, a rewarding association with New York University and an opportunity to enjoy its hospitality; second, it provided an occasion for attempting a brief interpretation of medical developments during the first two centuries of American experience.

Three of the four lectures were devoted to particular themes which, it was suggested, might appeal to as many, somewhat different audiences. This arrangement has both the advantages and the disadvantages of topical organization. Each topic necessarily overlaps at points with others, but an effort has been made to reduce repetition to the minimum essential to understanding. Within each lecture the analysis follows a roughly chronological sequence, and all three themes converge in the final chapter on the mid-nineteenth century.

Interest in the history of health and of medicine has increased markedly over the past generation, and the literature relating to the United States as well as that concerning other countries has grown accordingly. I am much indebted, as the citations will indicate, to many who have written in this field during the past thirty years. I also wish to acknowledge suggestions made, while the lectures were being prepared, by Dr. H. P. Tait and Dr. Douglas Guthrie of Edinburgh, by Dr. Whitfield J. Bell Jr. of the Benjamin Franklin Papers staff, and by Professor Brooke Hindle of New York University. My secretary, Mrs. Henry R. Marek, has been most helpful in typing the greater part of the manuscript.

No acknowledgments would be complete, finally, without reference to the unfailing courtesy extended by librarians—in London and in Edinburgh as well as in American cities—while the lectures were being prepared.

RICHARD H. SHRYOCK

The Library
American Philosophical Society
August, 1959

Contents

I

Origins of a Medical Profession

SOME fifty years ago scholars proclaimed a "new history" which was to emphasize a wide range of social developments. Such themes did receive increasing attention after that time but they were not so entirely "new" as was often assumed. Social history of some sort had appeared during the nineteenth century, to say nothing of still earlier manifestations. Much the same thing may be said of medical history in particular. Its social and professional aspects have been accorded marked recognition during recent decades, yet it would be a mistake to view this tendency as an altogether novel one. There had been writers, both historians and medical men, who displayed similar interests during the preceding century.

In 1839, for example, the demographer William Farr published an account of English professional developments and explained:

> The history of the English Medical Profession is here understood to imply the history of a social institution. . . . The state of Medical Science is only one of the elements of the inquiry; for the problem is—given a certain quantity of science, how has that science been brought into contact with people, by what class of persons, by what institutions, and with what effect? [1]

This statement so anticipates present interests that it might be used here as a guide in discussing the early American medical profession. Science, as Farr noted, is only one aspect of the story. A professional group is a product of the society in which it appears, as well as of its own tradition of learning. Such a guild influences and is influenced by that society as a whole and its history is largely the story of these relationships.

We now speak customarily of *the* medical profession as if there were only one; meaning, of course, the physicians. Nevertheless, a moment's thought about such other healing groups as veterinarians, dentists, druggists, opticians, midwives, nurses, and technicians—to say nothing of sectarians and quacks—will suggest that the present professional picture is not a simple one. Note also the subdivisions within these categories; for example, specialty bodies among physicians and the various types of nurses.

At first glance, the guild traditions inherited by early Americans seem less complicated. There were, in seventeenth- and eighteenth-century Europe, no technicians and few real dentists, veterinarians, or nurses, though sundry persons did work at corresponding trades. Even sectarians, in the present sense, were conspicuous by their absence. One aspect of the situation, however, may now appear confusing. This was the division of most medical practice between the three guilds of physicians, surgeons, and apothecaries. Confusion is increased by the fact that we still use the same designations, but with altered meanings.

One can explain most professional structure of that day in terms of these groups. More particularly, we are concerned with the British guilds, since they rather than the Continental provided the immediate background to American developments.[2] It is unnecessary to go into the history of the former other than to recall that by the eighteenth century each group possessed its own London College or Society and its own rights and privileges. The functions of one, nevertheless, sometimes overlapped those of another. Cooperation ensued in some instances, friction in others.

Physicians were the elite among medical men. Although sometimes apprenticed at the start, they usually attained university degrees and practiced largely among the upper classes. They were addressed as "doctor," whatever the degree. And, although they dealt with most kinds of illness, it would be misleading now to call them general practitioners. Perhaps internists would be the nearest, present term. Theoretically, as gentlemen and scholars, physicians did not work with their hands as did surgeons, nor should they engage in trade as did apothecaries. Although these distinctions were ignored in the provinces as impractical, they were maintained in the London area and to some extent in Edinburgh and other large towns. Such, in any case, were the ideals of the guild.

Surgeons were trained by apprenticeship and by hospital instruction, but rarely held degrees. Hence they were addressed—and still are in England—simply as "mister." They dealt chiefly with structural emergencies, superficial growths, and skin diseases. Such work was peripheral rather than central to the art of medicine. The services of surgeons were required on all social levels but their own status was inferior to that of physicians.

Apothecaries likewise lacked the standing of physicians. They were trained by apprenticeship and at times in hospital wards, although their London Society—like that of the surgeons—provided some instruction. Since they sold drugs, apothecaries eventually prescribed them as well, and so took on the role of general practitioners to the masses. Some apothecaries referred serious cases to physicians when available and the latter then served as consultants. It was assumed in time that apothecaries, as unlearned men, charged for their wares rather than for guidance—a distinction made legal in 1815. No doubt the arrangement tempted them to prescribe as much medicine as possible, with the result that Englishmen acquired a reputation abroad as "hard-dosing Islanders." Unfavorable portraits of apothecaries appeared in both eighteenth- and early nineteenth-century literature.[3]

Few, if any, guild distinctions were observed in rural areas and small towns. Medical men in these communities prescribed, sold drugs, and engaged in surgery. If they lacked degrees, they were sometimes called surgeon-apothecaries. In modern parlance, they could have been termed old-fashioned general practitioners.

There is little evidence that surgeons, apothecaries, or surgeon-apothecaries were interested in the latest theories of physicians or in the controversies these engendered. Apothecaries rarely published and surgeons wrote chiefly on technical matters. Both groups considered themselves practical men and expected to learn by experience. Apothecaries, it is true, were aware of traditional doctrines like that of humoralism and may have assumed them as a matter of course. But they were somewhat insulated from current aberrations in theory by the barriers separating them from physicians.

Parenthetically, one must not suppose that all physicians themselves were given to speculation. Many of them, by the eighteenth century, expressed a great respect for "facts" and some claimed to be empiricists. Most medical theories which seeped into the American colonies derived, as a matter of fact, from the one center of Edinburgh.

The licensing of British practitioners was a complex matter, not to be lingered over here. Procedures had changed over preceding centuries and had involved episcopal authorities, universities, and guild organizations. Separate arrangements were made in England, in Scotland, and in Ireland; and there were also distinct regulations within England for practice in London and in the provinces. It was assumed, however, that all reputable men were to be certified by some recognized authority.[4]

Such approval was occasionally expected even of midwives, though this group was of lowly status and can hardly be called a guild. They owed their trade largely to the moral taboo which, prior to about 1750, excluded male practitioners from obstetrics. One midwife doubtless learned from another but formal apprenticeships were uncommon. Some midwives were ignorant and uncouth, others were sensible persons who attained some skill. As a group they represented the sole exception to the rule that women had long been excluded from recognized medical practice in northern Europe.

Although licensing regulations had some value in labeling qualified practitioners, their enforcement was never such as to exclude folk healers, quacks, and charlatans from the scene. Quacks, like the poor, are always with us, and they exhibit common characteristics in all times and places. Hence, despite their picturesque behavior, we are tempted to dismiss them as constant factors in medical history. Actually, however, quackery does change with the times in relation to such factors as patent law and media of communication.

Printing, for example, encouraged the testimonials technique even before 1700, while patent law brought in patent medicines in the same era. And by the early eighteenth century newspaper and magazine advertising became available. Since medical men could do little in many cases, even the well-educated might turn to quacks in desperation. The difference between a real practitioner and a charlatan, indeed, might inhere more in motivations and fees than in the outcome. Hence it is not strange that quackery flourished in the colonies as well as in England during the eighteenth century. For that matter, it is with us today in somewhat subdued forms.

It is not easy to distinguish between quackery and self-medication. Most eighteenth-century folk apparently dosed themselves and consulted practitioners only when alarmed. The lower the income the more likely was this to be the case. Some chemist shops, competing with apothecaries, were already available; and it was here that a taste was acquired for "patent medicines." A number of the latter sold on a mass scale by the late 1700's—in the colonies as well as in the home country.[5]

In an effort to guide family practice, manuals were prepared in the vernacular by both medical men and laymen. Serious works, such as those of Tissot and Buchan, discussed hygiene as well as remedies and noted the dangers of quackery. This type of literature appeared in the United States before 1800 and sold widely under such titles as "the poor planter's friend" and "domestic companion." One of the most successful though not the most scientific of these efforts was the Rev. John Wesley's *Primitive Physic,* which went through some thirty editions in England and America between 1747 and

1858. Written originally for use by Methodists and intended to improve therapy for the masses, this work makes it clear enough that clerical practice was not unknown in England.[6]

The public had a great faith in medicines and such credulity was of advantage to apothecaries as well as to popular writers and quacks. There was, however, some distrust of licensed practitioners because of their secrecy and of their attempts to regulate practice. There was also a suspicion that even learned practice was pretentious and of little value. English satirists were not the equals of Molière but their intentions were similar. Thus Edward Baynard, in his "Doctor's Decade," revealed:

> In Ten Words the whole Art is comprised
> For some of the Ten are always advised . . .
> These few Evacuations
> Cure all the Doctor's Patients.
>
> What more they advance,
> Is all done by chance;
> So as to a Cure
> There's none to be sure.
>
> Most other Specificks
> Have no visible Effects,
> But the getting of Fees
> For a Promise of Ease. . . .[7]

One has in these lines an apt summary of the weaknesses of medical art at the time. Yet it is difficult to say how general such skepticism was. Other evidence suggests that most people who could afford it did resort at times to apothecaries or to physicians. Fashionable doctors were becoming affluent in the later 1700's. In present language, they had "never had it so good" as in this age of the gold-headed cane, and they naturally provided a social model for professional leaders in the colonies.

Such, in brief, was the professional situation in England and in Scotland during the first two centuries of American history. Why and to what extent did the picture change on this side of the Atlantic?

Among practitioners who came to the early settlements were a small number of physicians in the English sense, that is, men holding university degrees—sometimes the M.D. Taking Virginia as an example, however, Blanton states that only three or four such doctors are definitely known to have been resident prior to 1700. And Toner found that, over the next century, only one in nine of Virginia practitioners had received any formal training.[8] More common in the early colonies were "ships' surgeons" and others who had secured apprentice training and perhaps hospital experience abroad. These men, along with those who just began practicing without formalities, soon took on apprentices of their own—often under regular indentures. After the first generation such apprenticeship became the chief mode of education for those who had any pretension to professional status.

It need hardly be added that men so trained engaged in general practice, including surgery, dentistry, and the selling of drugs. And there were in most cases no consultants to whom serious cases could be referred. Hence it is usually said that English professional distinctions broke down or were deliberately abandoned in the presence of the American environment.

Now, London distinctions had no more place in rural America than they had in rural England. The larger colonial towns, on the other hand, were eventually able to support a number of real M.D.'s. But the latter, although educated abroad, were expected to practice just as other Americans did—including surgery and drug selling in their repertoire. One wonders, in passing, whether urban colonists would have preferred a differentiation of services along London lines.

The usual impression is that there was no such desire. For one thing, colonists were spared the rivalries of the guilds. Even city patients found it convenient, moreover, to secure complete attention from one family doctor. And the cost of his services was less, or at least seemed less, than would have been separate calls on separate guilds. Hence it may be held that the abandonment of London distinctions was fortunate. (Did not the mother country itself move in this direction during the next century?) Some American students agreed with this view when they first encountered the London guilds upon going there for further study. Thus Walter Channing, writing home as late as 1811, said there was too much emphasis upon [internal] medicine in Edinburgh and too much on surgery in London; but he thought the combination of the two fields among American practitioners was just right.

Yet there were advantages in the metropolitan arrangements. Notable were those inherent in specialization as such. In the first place, patients were more apt to know just what they were charged if they received a separate bill for drugs, rather than one from a general practitioner which might cover both medicines and fees. Other things being equal, moreover, a man engaged only in surgery was better qualified for such work than was a Jack-of-all-medical-trades. And a physician who did not handle drugs was enabled to give more time to other functions. These views, explicit in Dr. John Morgan's plans of 1765, continued to be advocated thereafter by various Americans. The same Walter Channing reversed his 1811 opinion nearly thirty-five years later. By that time he decided that specialization in surgery made for greater skill than was possessed by undifferentiated practitioners in the United States.[9]

The colonists never lost sight of one factor in the London physician's prestige: his formal education. A Virginia fee bill of 1736 actually discriminated in favor of those who possessed university degrees, and patients who could not find such persons occasionally wrote all the way to England for guidance. Young men who could afford it, meanwhile, risked the long voyage to Great Britain—along with the danger of smallpox—for the sake of formal training. Upon returning they were careful to make their degrees known and seem to have enjoyed greater prestige than did the home-grown personnel.

Friction between learned and unlearned medical men was rare, however, and arose only if the former made their sense of superiority too obvious. One interesting case of this sort was precipitated by controversy. In the bitter quarrel over inoculation at Boston in 1721, Dr. Douglass (the only M.D. in the city) attacked his opponent Boylston as an ignorant practitioner. To be specific, he referred to Boylston as "a certain cutter for stone" who lacked a degree. A group of clergymen immediately came to the defense not only of Boylston but of other local men as well. They declared that

> tho' he [Boylston] has not had the honour and advantages of an Academical Education, and consequently not the Letters of some Physicians in the Town, yet he ought by no means to be called Illiterate, ignorant, etc. Would the Town bear that Dr. Cutler or Dr. Davis should be so treated? [10]

The merits here attributed to apprenticed-trained personnel may have been real enough. But the clergy were, in any case, making a virtue of necessity. There were no other medical men, except Douglass himself, to whom they could turn. This situation, common everywhere before about 1730, continued to be the rule until after the Revolution except in the largest towns. It has been estimated that on the eve of that conflict there were about 3,500 established practitioners in the colonies and that not more than 400 of these had received any formal training. Of the latter, only about half—or barely more than 5 per cent of the total—held degrees.[11]

Why, in view of the prestige of the doctorate, did not more English M.D.'s settle in the colonies? In all probability, such men rarely came over for the simple reason that they were gentry and that upper classes in general did not emigrate. In early colonial days there were no opportunities worthy of their prestige; and by the late colonial epoch patterns of general practice had been set which most of them would not accept.[12] These patterns, after all, were similar to those of surgeon-apothecaries—a guild with which British physicians did not wish to be identified. The few who did migrate after 1730 were chiefly Scots, who fled from political or economic difficulties peculiar to their country and who often attained prominence in America.

The outcome in the colonies is usually said to have been a combining of the three English guilds into one. But it was not so simple as that, since physicians were long omitted in the American merger. Hence the story here was partly one of selective immigration rather than simply of adaptation to environment. There was no rejection of London distinctions in principle, nor was any new, native type of practice set up. All that happened was that few of the upper stratum of medical men came over, and that persons behaving like British surgeon-apothecaries (general practitioners) found themselves in consequence the sole colonial profession.

Then, much as merchants became aristocrats in the absence of a nobility, surgeon-apothecaries took on something of the status of physicians. The Americans, for example, began to be called "doctors," though very few held degrees. Blanton notes the usage as early as the seventeenth century,[13] and a reference to such doctors-by-courtesy in Boston (1721) has just been quoted.

Some form of address was needed but this hardly explains why the most exalted was chosen. *English* surgeons had to be content with "mister." In any case, more than a form of address was involved, since colonial practitioners were actually referred to as "physicians."[14] No doubt professional rank and file had no objection to such usage: it camouflaged the fact that Americans were served largely by men viewed in Europe as second-class personnel.

Once it is recognized that most American practitioners were really surgeon-apothecaries, the risks involved in comparing them with British (that is, London or Edinburgh) physicians become apparent. It may be misleading, for example, to say that American physicians sold drugs and that British physicians did not, when the reality was only that surgeon-apothecaries engaged in this trade on both sides of the Atlantic. Hence it might clarify matters if, for the period before 1765, we ceased to speak of American "physicians" altogether.

Old terminology persisted, of course, long after it had lost meaning. Colonists continued to refer to surgeons as if they were a distinct group. Indeed, the expression "physicians *and* surgeons" survived into our own time. The word "apothecary," on the other hand, held in the colonies to its original connotation of "druggist," and was little employed as long as medicines were dispensed chiefly by practitioners. When a few druggists appeared in the larger towns after about 1760 they were termed either apothecaries or chemists. Such men did not encroach on practice, except that some performed routine bleeding for a modest fee.

Distinctions between guilds were the more easily forgotten because there were no licensing regulations. The lack of such rules is not surprising in a rural society where there were no institutions to provide standards. Yet something could conceivably have been done by provincial officials if there had been a demand for it in the larger towns. In Peru (1569) and Mexico (1570) the early protomedicatos were supposed to license all practitioners and even to distinguish between the traditional guilds. In these respects the medical code of Castile was applied to the American viceroyalties;[15] but there was no analogy to this action in the case of English colonies.

In the first place, the English concept of medical police was a more limited one than that which developed in more paternalistic societies. And such as they were, the English regulations were not projected into the colonies. London left such matters to the provinces themselves. By the early nineteenth century Continental writers viewed British medical-police codes as backward and American as nonexistent.[16]

Authorities in the English colonies did not forget the licensing tradition altogether and at times displayed an uneasy feeling that something should be done about it. During the mid-seventeenth century, for example, the Massachusetts General Court provided that practitioners must be approved by those wise in medical matters. Such a program was as vague as it was well intended. Subsequently, moreover, no efforts were made to hold examinations and licensing was in effect abandoned—not only in the Bay Province but in all the colonies.

How far the idea of social control was lost, even while paternalistic attitudes still obtained to some degree in the economic sphere, is suggested by the fact that men were occasionally licensed *after* they had attained prominence as practitioners. Such was the case with the Rev. Gershow Bulkeley, who was so recognized by the Connecticut Assembly in 1686.[17] Here the license was transformed into a sort of honorary degree.

It is doubtful if licensing controls could ever have been effective as long as there were few well-trained medical men. At the time, however, some observers thought this causal relationship could be reversed: that licensing in itself would assure a supply of better practitioners. The New York historian William Smith, in an oft-quoted passage of 1757, stated: "Few Physicians amongst us are eminent for their skill. Quacks abound like locusts in *Egypt*. . . . This is less to be wondered at as the profession is under no kind of Regulation. Any man at his pleasure sets up for Physician, Apothecary, and Chirurgen."[18]

As Smith implied, there was no dearth in well-settled communities of persons who called themselves doctors. If the estimated number of practitioners for 1775 is correct, and if we assume a total population of 2 million, the ratio of so-called doctors to population was about 1:600 in the Revolutionary era. This is a high national proportion by modern standards, but the surplus was even greater in the towns. Using data cited by Bell for New York in 1750, we arrive at a ratio of about 1:350; and for Williamsburg in 1730 at the startling figure of 1:135.[19]

Under these circumstances average returns from practice were probably low; but this did not mean that the income of the more successful medical men was in that category. Charges for drugs, parenthetically, at times bulked larger than fees in medical bills—the usual situation in an apothecary's practice. The busy Dr. Hugh Mercer of Fredericksburg, for example, was charging, by the early seventies, 5 shillings for a visit but no less than 7/6 for doses of galap—the latter figure being about the price of two pairs of shoes.[20] No wonder that when one Dr. James McClurg rejected the functions of both surgeon and apothecary, he could not make a living; and that simply an abstention from drug selling aroused professional resentment against Dr. Adam Thompson at Philadelphia in 1748.[21]

Apart from charges for medicines, the chief basis for the remuneration of colonial practitioners was the traditional fee for service. There may have been occasional contract practice with families or with planters for the care of their slaves—an old prepayment scheme by which an annual charge covered all fees. But such arrangements were not common enough to change the general pattern. Payments might be made in money, in products like tobacco which passed for money, or simply on a barter basis.

Also traditional—perhaps medieval in origin—was the assumption that practitioners should provide free treatment or reduced rates to the poor, securing compensation through higher than average charges to the wealthy. Whether colonial practitioners also gave "courtesy" (free) service to one another (as did English physicians) is not clear, though this procedure probably emerged later with the development of an organized profession.

In any case, these arrangements have all survived in this country to the present time. In themselves they involve an unusual social pattern—particularly in the assumption that a guild shares at its own discretion in the responsibilities of poor relief. The "sliding scale" of fees involved has in recent years been subjected to serious criticism on economic grounds.[22]

One should recall, on the other hand, that medical men themselves faced difficulties in trying to combine traditional altruism with high charges to the wealthy. Just because medical services were viewed as transcending ordinary business arrangements, unusual demands were made on the "doctors"—particularly in rural practice. And it seems to have been assumed, even by the prosperous, that payment of medical bills was not a pressing matter. The practitioner, as the friend of the family, would understand. But the former suspected that patients lost interest in payments as soon as they were well. Complaints on this score were proverbial on both sides of the Atlantic. As Pope put it:

God and the Doctor we alike adore,
But only when in danger, not before;
The danger over, both are alike requited,
God is forgotten and the Doctor slighted.[23]

One of the difficulties presented by a sliding scale of fees was that of determining a fair charge under any particular circumstances. Apart from health regulations, most colonial medical legislation and court actions concerned financial relationships between practitioner and patient. Provincial annals are full of patients' protests about fees and about the price of drugs, but they also include practitioners' suits for payment. Interrelated with financial issues were occasional charges of negligence or malpractice. In general, colonial laws sought to keep fees on a reasonable level and to provide for cancellation and censure when they were excessive. But the courts at the same time recognized the right to collect fair charges.[24]

It would be interesting to know whether patients ever engaged medical men on a contingency basis. Such procedure was followed occasionally by local authorities, who were unwilling to use public funds for poor relief unless results were guaranteed. If no cure was effected, payment might be reduced or denied altogether. In 1667, for example, Christ Church Parish in Virginia offered to pay 5,000 pounds of tobacco provided a "perfect cure" was made in the case of "Jno. Blake, a poor decrepit Man of this Parish."[25] Analogous procedure is used to this day in law, and more than one unhappy patient has wished that it could be revived in medical circles.

The low average return from medical practice is explained by the surplus of practitioners, but this surplus in turn can be ascribed to the fact that many persons worked only part time "at doctoring" and so had other sources of income. What probably happened was that, in early settlements, there was a dearth of medical personnel of any sort, so that families turned to all and sundry who thought themselves qualified. Individuals thereupon began to practice on the side, and at some point the original famine in personnel was replaced by a surfeit. In old communities, thereafter, even apprentice-trained men might have to take on other work in order to make ends meet.

It was not uncommon to farm, preach, practice law, or indulge in other activities on the side. Even indentured servants or slaves occasionally enjoyed local reputations as healers. And there seems to have been little objection at first to medical women, not only as midwives but also as "doctresses" at large. Cotton Mather, aware of professional opposition abroad, defended the ability of their sex in this sphere and instructed his own daughter in the healing art.[26] Women as general practitioners, however, seem to have dropped out of the picture during the early eighteenth century—perhaps because more apprentice-trained men were becoming available.

Women also acted as nurses but this function was more commonly performed by men. In the Protestant environment of the English colonies there were no nursing orders of either sex. Lay nurses, or "keepers," were untrained, self-appointed persons whose duties were custodial rather than medical in nature. They sometimes served in addition as undertakers, in which capacity they were responsible for wakes or other funeral arrangements to which the colonists were addicted. Nothing beyond such services was envisaged in this country until well into the nineteenth century, although efforts to train lay nurses were made in Germany as early as the 1770's.[27] The advent of the first American hospitals does not seem to have changed the situation. Benjamin Rush's attitude was probably typical when he praised individual nurses but viewed their craft as a menial one.

American midwives were indistinguishable from their British counterparts. All obstetrical practice was in their hands until after the mid-eighteenth century. Although lacking even formal apprenticeship in most cases, some of them were quite reputable persons. Since they rarely interfered with births, their practice may have been safer in some respects than was that of later physicians. But their methods were based on folklore and they had little knowledge to fall back on in difficult cases.

The most impressive types of lay practice were those conducted by planters, magistrates, and clergymen. In a day when educated persons were still familiar with medical literature the line between lay and professional status was vague at best. Indeed, a man who had graduated from an arts college, read in medicine, and acquired some experience was the nearest thing to a formally trained practitioner that the colonial environment produced before the 1760's. As late as about 1830, it may be added, the University of Virginia still provided instruction in medicine for all its undergraduate students.

A few of the clerical practitioners, such as Henry M. Muhlenberg of Pennsylvania and Jared Eliot of Connecticut, were very able men.[28] And they could acquire experience as readily as the next man. Such experience was encountered in calls on sick parishioners, and some clergymen never went further than this incidental, parochial care. It was most common when respectable, full-time practitioners were not available. But other ministers, intrigued by medicine, gave it serious attention and indulged in genuine clerical practice.

A patient who could choose between one of these clergymen and an ordinary village "doc" may have found the decision difficult. Admittedly, from the present viewpoint, neither type was apt to know much about science: the favorite remedies of the Rev. Mr. Bulkeley were acquired by him from a Hartford blacksmith! But the minister, in view of his education and mission, may have inspired the greater confidence.

Apprentice-trained "doctors," however, have had their defenders. Oliver Wendell Holmes, writing about 1860, looked back on them as sound empiricists, uncorrupted by theoretical nonsense. (But in another essay, curiously enough, he ridiculed the so-called "practical men" of his own time.) [29] And today some nostalgia for "the old family doctor"—based perhaps on the 1850–1900 version—may project certain virtues back into the eighteenth-century setting. In any case, few of the ordinary practitioners of the 1700's left records and most surviving comments on them came from men of superior education.

European-trained leaders of the eighteenth century, conscious of their superior background, were certainly severe in criticisms of the rank and file. Dr. Douglass, in a work published in 1753, declared that common practice was "perniciously bad" and added:

> Frequently there is *more Danger* from the Physician, than from the Distemper . . . but sometimes notwithstanding the Male *Practice,* Nature gets the better of the Doctor, and the Patient recovers.[30]

Equally aggressive in condemnation was Dr. John Morgan, who in 1765 stated that many people received no aid from medical science and that even large towns harbored practitioners who were in "a pitiful state of ignorance" concerning their profession. Warming to his subject, Morgan described the havoc wrought by these unscientific men and appealed to them to hold their exterminating hands! [31]

Morgan was arguing for formal education and so may have overstated his case. It is now a truism that apprentice training had certain practical values if the preceptor was an able and conscientious man. But how often was this the case? The literature of the late 1700's and early 1800's contains many complaints on this score: on the monotonous and uninspiring nature of apprenticeships. Training of this sort was tolerated by some good men, but anyone who could read and write was eligible to receive it.

It would seem, then, that colonial practitioners were a miscellaneous lot. Many were no better at the end of the eighteenth century. Looking back from 1818, for example, Dr. John Stearns—president of the New York Medical Society—declared that scientific knowledge had been restricted to the largest cities until the state societies were formed. Stearns added: "With a few, honorable exceptions in each city, the practitioners were ignorant, degraded and contemptible." [32] This indictment, in merely mentioning the "honorable exceptions," failed to bring out certain marked improvements which will be noted shortly. But, assuming even its partial truth, one can understand why—in Benjamin Rush's words—the medical profession had long held only "a slavish rank" in American society.[33]

In thinking of the colonial era one tends to foreshorten the time perspective. It is difficult to realize, for example, that Virginia—even now—has been an American state no longer than it was an English province. To be more specific, a Virginian looking back from 1730 to the original settlement, was recalling an interval as lengthy as we would now recall in harking back to 1836. Yet for about that span, 1607 to 1730, colonial medical practice had been conducted on the relatively primitive levels just described.

It is a temptation to paint the early picture in even darker hues than it merits, by way of contrast to the progress that ensued. For there was progress after about 1730, not so much in science but rather in professional and institutional developments. In these respects a dawning enlightenment in medicine paralleled the quite different Great Awakening in religion during the middle decades of the eighteenth century. A few medical institutions and at least a nascent medical profession were permanently established in the colonies by the 1760's.

Circumstances on both sides of the Atlantic converged to make this outcome possible. In eighteenth-century Europe scientific advances made medicine more exciting to contemporaries than it now appears to us. Even the speculations set off by these developments were evidences of ferment. New knowledge, meantime, stimulated medical teaching in a relatively empirical environment and the standards of medical education rose successively at Leyden, Edinburgh, and London.

It was to these centers in about that order that American medical students migrated after 1730 in search of real professional training. Whether European physicians would come over or not, Americans would go abroad and return as first-class medical men themselves. Thus they inaugurated what Dixon Ryan Fox later called a stage in the transit of culture.

Ostensibly these young men studied medical science and its applications to practice. But they observed a great deal more: other lands and other ways, professional guilds, societies, publications, and hospitals. Could not similar institutions be established in the colonies? Medicine often appealed simultaneously to a man's scientific curiosity and to his desire to do good, and now there was added the prospect of serving one's province or even one's country at large. The latter motivation became stronger with the Revolution, but it was there earlier in at least incipient form.[34]

American students, whatever their ideals, were not visionaries. The very fact that their families could send them abroad was evidence of an expanding economy and of rising standards of living at home. Colonial cities were now comparable, in population and wealth, with provincial cities in the mother country. Material prosperity was associated with a more secular spirit in America as well as in Europe, and the needs of the mind as well as those of the body received increasing attention. Philadelphia, by the late 1760's, even possessed an American Philosophical (scientific) Society modeled on the Royal Society of London. In such a setting, low professional standards could no longer be tolerated without protest. Thus the native urban environment, as well as the European, played its role in medical awakening.[35]

Europeans who held degrees had criticized American professional arrangements even before 1730. One recalls Dr. Douglass' scorn of Boston practitioners in 1721 and also his resentment against clerics who still meddled in medicine. During ensuing decades, as noted, immigrant doctors occasionally tried to practice as physicians but usually ended by conforming to the American pattern. Nevertheless, by about the 1760's opportunities for genteel practice were expanding in large towns and educational standards were rising. Partially in response to these circumstances, more young men were returning with foreign degrees, and they in turn took the initiative in urging firmer foundations for a learned profession.

A few of these men envisaged the possibility of limiting all practice to genuine physicians—hardly a realistic program at that time. Bell has pointed out that Arthur Lee and other Virginians at Edinburgh proposed, in 1765, that their Assembly should limit future admission to medical practice to those holding an M.D. Other Americans probably assumed that physicians would be superimposed, as an elite, on the mass of general practitioners—a fulfillment of British tradition which corresponded to the actual situation evolving in colonial cities.

Implicit in these alternatives was an issue which, although basic, is easily overlooked. British guild arrangements provided for learned doctors but room was left for the half-trained—to say nothing of those with even lesser pretensions. No one group held a monopoly, and licensing served more to define guild distinctions than to keep unlearned persons from practicing in one way or another. In a word, medicine had remained a largely open field. This situation blended well with the relatively free economy of the British Empire, but it also involved much low-grade practice among the people at large.

Now, the most obvious scheme for providing first-class medical care to the entire public was to require, presumably by such government sanctions as Lee suggested, that all practitioners meet the requirements for physicians. But this procedure would, in effect, constitute a demand for a professional monopoly; and monopolies were—and still are—suspect in free societies.[36] If disinterested social reformers had urged such a program, it could have been debated on its merits. But when, as actually occurred, it was physicians themselves who finally advocated a monopoly, they were inevitably suspected of masking their own interests under the guise of public welfare.

Efforts to raise requirements for all practitioners characterized both British and American professional history for 150 years after 1760. They were always countered, at least in the United States, by a defense of laissez-faire competition and an attack on the motivations of medical men. For such physicians as were really concerned about public welfare the situation was a frustrating one. In their favor was the fact that the effort to raise requirements began only when scientific advances indicated some superiority in the practice of well-educated men. And ultimately the drive would be successful only when science made such superiority an undeniable one.

In the 1760's this long, historical process was just getting under way in the English colonies.[37] It took its particular form from the provincial relationship to England, but, as elsewhere, it was inextricably entwined with other aspects of professional improvement —with the development of medical institutions of all kinds. The whole story is best illustrated by developments in Philadelphia, which was then becoming the chief American medical center.

Philadelphia, by 1760 the largest city in the colonies, had never been dominated by any one church or its clergy. There may have been disadvantages in this, as in the delay in founding colleges; but a secular atmosphere prevailed from the start and medicine could flourish as well therein as could divinity. Able Welsh practitioners had come out with Penn, but the real advent of the Quaker City medical tradition may be symbolized by the career of Dr. John Kearsley, Sr., who had arrived in 1711 after "a good medical education in England."

Kearsley had trained by apprenticeship such men as John Redman, John Bard, and the two Bonds. Redman, in turn, was preceptor, at mid-century, to the distinguished practitioners of the Revolutionary era—Morgan, Rush, and Wistar. Redman, as well as Kearsley before him, was a product of European education; and apprenticeship with such men was more valuable than that with home-grown practitioners. It not only was superior in itself but it encouraged students to study abroad even as had their masters.[38]

There were, of course, individual leaders in other cities who were as promising as those in Philadelphia, but as a group the latter were outstanding by 1760. Indeed, the sequence from Kearsley to the Bonds and Redman and then from the latter to Rush and Morgan was a preceptorial succession of great promise in American medicine.

On this line hung, first, the institutional developments in which Philadelphians pioneered. Notable was the founding of the Pennsylvania Hospital in 1751, chiefly by Dr. Thomas Bond with the cooperation of Benjamin Franklin. There had been "pest houses" and domiciliary care of the sick long before that, and the almshouses at Boston and Philadelphia were "hospitals" in the old sense. But the Pennsylvania was the first English-American hospital in the modern meaning of the word. Similar to it was the New York Hospital, which Dr. Samuel Bard envisaged in the sixties and "founded" in 1771—though it did not get fully under way until 1791.

Hence, except for brief attempts made in Virginia during the early 1600's, one may say that hospitals proper did not appear until more than a century after the first settlements. In Spanish and French colonies the Church set up such institutions more promptly. But the Anglican and nonconformist English churches had given up the hospital tradition, and state or "voluntary" agencies acted only under the cumulative pressures of public need, secular humanitarianism, and professional initiative.

The Pennsylvania Hospital was an interesting one in several ways apart from the fact that it happened to be the first. Although granted some provincial funds, it was set up under voluntary auspices and was governed by a private, self-perpetuating board. Here was the same pattern that was employed with English and American colleges, in contrast to the European habit of placing philanthropic institutions in the hands of church or state.

The Pennsylvania was modeled on British voluntary hospitals and was intended primarily to care for the sick poor regardless of residence. But, unlike most British institutions, it admitted some private patients to whom attending doctors charged fees. The presence of such persons may have maintained upper-class interest in the hospital and thus made for higher standards than those often found in strictly charitable institutions. The Pennsylvania also benefited from the practical idealism of Quaker leadership. Between 1751 and 1773 it housed an average of about 400 patients a year, with only some 39 deaths among them—a mortality rate of about 10 per cent. European hospital mortality was said to average around double that figure. There is no doubt that the Pennsylvania was superior to most hospitals of the time, but it had its counterparts in some of the better European institutions.[39]

Although practitioners who attended in almshouses were paid, professional leaders appointed to the Pennsylvania served in the wards without compensation. These posts carried prestige from the start, and the staff—in modern parlance—were all "part-time men." Borrowed from English usage, this arrangement has been maintained ever since for a large proportion of medical personnel in voluntary hospitals.

Financial arrangements with practitioners, however, precipitated an issue which was inherent in the management of the Pennsylvania—or of any nonprofit institution—by a lay board. Should this body exercise complete control or should it share policy decisions with the staff of experts? The latter, of course, were consulted, and things apparently went smoothly until 1783. Then, when the Pennsylvania staff charged fees for some almshouse patients given special service, almshouse officials objected and the hospital board rescinded the fees. This outraged the doctors involved and John Morgan resigned from the service in protest. He may have expected that the board would give in to the staff but the former held its ground.[40] No doubt the board was within its legal rights; but the issue between trustees and medical staff would come up again in later hospital history—sometimes with the opposite result.

Besides serving both the poor and private patients, the Pennsylvania was intended to offer training facilities to medical students. Franklin, who was presumably familiar with such arrangements abroad, pointed out this purpose during the original campaign for funds. And Thomas Bond did give clinical lectures at the hospital after 1765.

Even before that, however, the younger Dr. Shippen offered private lectures on anatomy and midwifery upon returning to Philadelphia in 1762. (He had been trained under Dr. Smellie in London and was heir to the best British tradition in obstetrics.) Similar private lectures were given in London and Edinburgh, perhaps as an outgrowth of the apprentice system. But Shippen anticipated that his courses would evolve, with additional support, into a full-fledged medical school. Meantime he admitted midwives as well as medical apprentices, and the former could receive separate instruction if they desired.

The potential significance of Shippen's work with midwives and of Samuel Bard's similar efforts in New York has not always been fully appreciated. These men apparently assumed that, with better instruction, midwives could take care of many cases and that emergencies could be referred to qualified physicians. For thirty years or more after 1762 one finds occasional "ads" in newspapers by women claiming superior training under Shippen. Had this program been continued, it might eventually have paralleled that later development in European countries. Instead, after the 1780's, medical men gradually and permanently replaced midwives except among the poorest classes.

Thus women were, in a sense, driven from their last bastion in American medical practice. All this was done under the plea that physicians were safer because better informed. Whether true or not, this argument had no bearing on what might have been accomplished *if* the midwives had been better trained. Just why the subsequent history of American midwifery ran such a different course from the European never seems to have been adequately explained.

The establishment of the first American medical school is an oft-told tale, and we need not repeat here the parts taken by Shippen the younger and by John Morgan or the bitter rivalry which arose between the two men. But the fact that the planning was first done at Edinburgh, by colonial students there, is a significant one. Had the scheme taken form in London, it might have led to the founding of a hospital-school in the wards of the Pennsylvania. But with the University of Edinburgh in mind, Morgan persuaded the College of Philadelphia to set up a medical faculty in 1765 and so introduced the Continental-Scottish tradition of a university-college.

This tradition was lost in many later schools, but since about 1915 American institutions have returned to it in large measure.

The first medical school in the colonies was an immediate success, and its founding was the one instance in which Dr. Morgan's plans came to full fruition within his own lifetime. The original faculty consisted only of Morgan (theory and practice) and Shippen (anatomy and surgery); but Adam Kuhn was added in botany and materia medica in 1768 and Rush in chemistry in '69. Moreover, Provost William Smith lectured in natural philosophy (physical science) and Thomas Bond gave what were in effect clinical lectures for the school. At least one year's course of lectures after apprenticeship were required for the M.B. Three years thereafter a man could defend a thesis and qualify for an M.D., though few actually took that degree until after the baccalaureate was abolished in 1789. In terms of both curriculum and staff, the school was a progressive one by European standards.

The same was true of the King's College medical school organized in New York in 1768, largely through the efforts of Dr. Samuel Bard. Both New York and Philadelphia schools were later disorganized by the Revolution. The former was closed for years, until reorganized in 1792; and a rival school was founded by the so-called University of New York in 1807, with such able professors as David Hosack, Edward Miller, and Samuel L. Mitchill. In Philadelphia, also, a second school was established in the 1780's by the patriot-inspired University of the State of Pennsylvania. But the two Philadelphia colleges were joined in 1791, and the two New York institutions united in 1813. Since then they have had an uninterrupted history as, respectively, the medical schools of the University of Pennsylvania and of Columbia University.

Medical institutions appeared somewhat later in Boston. Men with Edinburgh degrees had taken the initiative in the earlier ones, but there were few such doctors in the Boston area. In 1780, however, John Warren lectured on anatomy in a Continental army hospital at Cambridge, and three years later he persuaded Harvard College to set up a medical school. No real hospital was available at first for instructional purposes and Harvard students had to make the best of facilities at the Boston Almshouse. (In 1810, however, the Harvard school moved into Boston, where the Massachusetts General Hospital was opened in 1821.) Hence by the end of the eighteenth century the three largest American cities possessed medical schools connected with arts colleges, and the future of medical education seemed bright.[41]

In founding the first medical school Dr. Morgan had had more in mind than a strong faculty and curriculum. The chief purpose of the school was to provide more Americans with access to professional education but not all comers were to be welcomed. Only those with a preliminary academic training should be admitted—another idea later abandoned in this country and revived only after 1893. Graduates would raise professional standards throughout the country; first, by virtue of superior learning and, second, by practicing only as physicians. In other words, they would eschew surgery and drug selling.

Today, despite common medical school backgrounds, the practice of surgery *has* become a distinctive one and pharmacy does involve an independent profession. Hence Morgan's argument for separating these guilds, like his demand for premedical training, may be viewed as almost prophetic in 1765.[42]

But other factors seem to have influenced the Philadelphian's outlook. For one thing, he prized the social distinction then implicit in the very concept of a physician. He pointed out that, just as generals did not dig trenches, so physicians need not perform the less dignified tasks of medical practice. As he put it:

> Where a proper subordination is wanting, there is a perversion of all practical knowledge. No more then is a physician obliged, from his office, to handle a knife with a surgeon; to cull herbs with the botanist; . . . or to compound drugs with the apothecary.[43]

Moreover, progressive as Morgan's argument seems from the present standpoint, it was at the time largely an appeal to introduce superior British practice into the colonies. Few of his ideas were really new but they took on a progressive quality in the American setting. The best medicine was to be practiced in Philadelphia much as it was in metropolitan London.

Morgan's program was a comprehensive one. Training worthy of physicians was to be provided (premedical education, a graded curriculum) and graduates were to practice only *as* physicians (eschewing surgery and drug selling). Meantime they were to be set apart by examinations and licensing and they would control these procedures through their own organizations. No more complete scheme for "medical reform" was presented in this country until Billings, Welch, Osler, and others inaugurated the Hopkins program in the 1890's.[44]

The most novel aspect of Morgan's plan lay in its implications for the professional control of practice. He did not go so far as to demand an immediate monopoly for physicians. He may have assumed that surgeons would continue to be prepared simply by apprenticeship, and he did not say explicitly that "doctors" trained only in that same manner should be banned from practice. But his bitter criticism of such practitioners, combined with his demand for the licensing of real physicians, seemed to imply that the latter might take over all internal medicine when this became feasible. In other words, he showed no desire to perpetuate the British tradition of second-class, general practitioners, but never thought out just what was to be done with them. In this respect he dimly foreshadowed the efforts to eliminate personnel of this sort that would characterize European and American professional history during the ensuing century.

Within the limits noted, the Philadelphian's plan for professional restrictions was an interesting one. He hoped to found an elite college of physicians, on the London model, which would license physicians on an intercolonial scale. Appeals for licensing of some sort were becoming more common by this time but these usually postulated control by state courts or other official agencies.[45] Morgan, conversely, preferred to keep the function, as in England, in the hands of professional bodies. His scheme for control centered in Philadelphia was doubtless unrealistic, but seems to have been the first intercolonial gesture in medical circles. Note that it was concomitant with early plans for political cooperation and even for a political union among the colonies.

Unfortunately for Morgan, the scheme for a licensing authority met with immediate opposition. Provost Smith feared that it would interfere with the Medical Department of the College of Philadelphia. And Dr. Fothergill, in London, criticized the plan as implying a monopoly—with the result that Thomas Penn, the proprietor, refused to grant a charter.

As will be noted, other licensing programs were adopted in 1766 and ensuing years, but they differed in form in the various provinces or states and none attempted to eliminate practitioners trained only by apprenticeship. Indeed, the few medical schools in existence prior to 1820 could not possibly have met the need for medical personnel if any such demand had been made upon them. The outcome in this country was a situation not unlike that overseas, with graduates of three or four medical schools corresponding roughly to British physicians and the rank-and-file practitioners to British surgeon-apothecaries.

Meantime the failure to charter a college of physicians was a double blow to Morgan, since he had expected the institution to serve the additional function of encouraging research. Here, again, one notes the man's insight. He seems to have realized that in the long run the claim of physicians to guild superiority could be best justified by expanding scientific knowledge and so widening the gap between them and the "mere empirics." But here he encountered indifference among even those who held degrees, most of whom were absorbed in practice. At best, they envisaged research only in terms of occasional clinical or epidemiologic reports on certain diseases.

The lack of research in this period may be ascribed in part to social circumstances; notably to the popular aversion to human dissection. That procedure was not only basic in medical education but was essential to studies in pathologic anatomy—a field which was becoming by 1800 the medical science par excellence. How violent public attitudes could be was illustrated by the notorious "Doctors' Mob" at New York City in 1788, when a crowd attempted to lynch those engaged in dissections.[46] Hence physicians had to rob graveyards for teaching purposes and permission for autopsies could rarely be secured.

More than social obstacles, however, was involved in this situation. There was some opposition to research in principle, even in medical circles. Would not investigations, pursued perhaps out of sheer curiosity, distract a man from his first duty to patients? Morgan's old preceptor, Redman, wrote him in effect that physicians were too busy for original studies. Far better was it that they should be "doing good to rich and poor." Indeed, declared Dr. Redman, "No life can be happy or pleasing to God but what is useful to man." [47] The implication that research would not be useful to practitioners was clear enough. This view had often been expressed before and was difficult to refute in the 1760's—or for many decades thereafter. And it must be admitted that Morgan himself subsequently failed to practice what he preached in this regard.

On the theme of Dr. Morgan's frustrations it may be added that his efforts to eliminate surgery and drug selling from the physician's practice also seemed fruitless. After his death in 1789 a few medical men—among whom Dr. Physick was outstanding—began to emphasize surgery but did not limit their practice to it. Complete specialization in this field did not emerge until nearly a century later, under circumstances radically different from those of 1765. As for drugs, some doctors continued selling them into the present century.

In retrospect one can see that Dr. Morgan's efforts in regard to licensing, research, and forms of practice were somewhat premature. The Philadelphia environment, for all its promise, was not the equivalent of that of London; nor, by the same token, was that of any other American city. If this were the entire story, one could picture the chief actor as a farseeing but quixotic figure: as one who was typically "ahead of his time." Yet the story is not really as simple as that. Although apparently blocked by social and professional inertia, Morgan sensed correctly that changes were imminent and he did "start something" in more than one respect.

Consider, first, the matter of drug selling. It is true that the medical reformer was himself reduced, in time and in some degree, to practice of this sort. But there is evidence that urban doctors gradually abandoned that practice during the decades between 1790 and 1820. The trend was feasible only as cities grew and "apothecaries and druggists" became more numerous. And when this occurred a new problem arose, in that the druggists of 1820 were as casually trained as most "doctors" had been in the 1760's.[48] Nevertheless, Morgan had pointed the way.

Consider, also, Morgan's activities in organizing professional bodies which would lend cohesion as well as prestige to the guild. Here he was not strictly a pioneer, for a short-lived medical society had appeared in Boston as early as the 1730's. Several similar bodies were formed during the mid-sixties and in 1766 the pioneer state (provincial) society was set up in New Jersey. In that same year Morgan was active in forming the Philadelphia Medical Society and he hoped that this would evolve into his college of physicians. When the latter was blocked, Morgan and his fellow members helped to reorganize and were absorbed into the American Philosophical Society. That society encouraged scientific studies and so pursued in a general way one of the objectives which Morgan had had in mind.[49]

Finally, the College of Physicians of Philadelphia *was* founded in 1787—largely through the efforts of Rush but fulfilling in part Dr. Morgan's original plan. The college, although it never played a role in licensing, did take some interest in research and established the second institutional medical library in the country (1788)—the first having been that set up in the Pennsylvania Hospital (1762). The College, admitting members only by election, afforded prestige within a learned profession on a national scale.[50]

Meantime the Revolution had delayed the formation of state medical societies similar to the New Jersey group of 1766. But within a decade after the end of hostilities such bodies were organized in five other states; and by 1815 nearly all states possessed them.[51] The immediate goals of medical societies were to set better-qualified practitioners apart from others by licensing provisions and to seek harmony within the superior guild by personal contacts and by a voluntary regulation of competition. The need for some degree of harmony, if a real profession was to be established, was apparent to certain leaders in the 1760's and became painfully obvious by the nineties.

Lacking even the guild restraints of European societies, competition in practice was a free-for-all in this country. The uncertainties of medical science also made for friction between practitioners over matters vital to the public as well as to the guild. Physicians, in both Europe and America, bickered among themselves and at times engaged in open controversies. In consequence they became known as a quarrelsome lot and this did not help the reputation of the profession.

Even the leading men were involved not only in ordinary competition but also in rivalry for institutional prestige. Philadelphia may serve again as an example. In the first medical school Morgan and Shippen were such enemies that it is a wonder the faculty held together. Shippen's role in the original planning had been deliberately hidden, he believed, when Morgan claimed all the credit. Their quarrel was intensified by controversy over the medical services during the Revolutionary War and the outcome almost ruined the careers of both men.

Rush, subsequently, became involved in similar recriminations—in his case, over scientific issues. In the course of the yellow fever epidemics he accused some doctors of ineffective treatments and of letting their patients die in consequence. But his rivals declared that *he* was the one who was killing patients with excessive bleedings and purgings. Rush's remedy, said his colleague Kuhn, was "a murderous dose," and a Dr. Hodge declared it "a dose for a horse"! Both parties carried their accusations into the newspapers, and the public took sides. Late in life, perhaps with this bitter experience in mind, Rush urged an end to quarrels over scientific matters; and he added that "the whole odium of the hostility of physicians to each other" should be ascribed to nothing more than "competition for business and money."[52]

In order to minimize friction, medical societies had discussed professional conduct as early as the 1760's. Indeed, Dr. Samuel Bard published a *Discourse upon the Duties of Physicians* in 1769. But not until Thomas Percival brought out his *Medical Ethics* in London, in 1803, was a detailed code available to English-speaking practitioners. This code dealt more with etiquette than with ethics, and so had more bearing on guild interests than on those of the public. The latter were not entirely ignored, however. Percival, for example, justified criticism of one physician's practice by another in cases involving ignorance or neglect—a principle which seems to have been forgotten in present professional attitudes toward malpractice suits. Codes based on Percival's were published in the United States in the 1820's and similar ones were subsequently adopted by various medical societies.[53]

Since disputes over bills had been responsible for much friction between doctors and patients, fee codes or "bills" intended to set fair charges had been included in colonial legislation. Such action may be interpreted in terms of the economic paternalism of the early period. By the 1760's, however, practitioners revived the guild idea of a regulation of fees by practitioners themselves. They realized, as did many a trade thereafter, that sharp competition in prices might be injurious to all who provided service—whatever the advantages to consumers. In the case of medicine it could be argued that harmony among practitioners had some values even for the public.

Medical societies therefore adopted fee bills to which their members agreed to conform. That of the New Jersey Society, drawn up in 1766, was probably typical of those subsequently set up by other societies. It listed charges of 25 cents and up for country calls according to mileage and as much as $3.50 for deliveries. In terms of current values, these were substantial charges.[54]

Rounding out its program, the New Jersey Society persuaded the provincial legislature of 1772 to provide licensing restrictions and to establish a provincial examination board. This board, except for local provisions made in New York City (1760), was the first such agency in the country. The precedent it established was subsequently followed by most states during the half century between 1780 and 1830; that is, licensing procedures of some sort were thereafter provided.

During this era, which we would now view as transitional, it was still assumed that most candidates for a license would not be medical graduates. Hence, in order to introduce standards among such men, regulations concerning apprenticeship as well as examinations were provided. A New York City law of 1792, for example, required that candidates lacking a college education must serve an apprenticeship of three years with a reputable practitioner. Candidates holding an arts degree need serve only two years, while those who were medical graduates were exempted from all these requirements.[55] Actually, however, apprenticeship long remained the rule even among those men who subsequently secured a medical degree.

It is difficult to say how effectively regulations on apprenticeship were enforced or just what standards were maintained by the early examining boards. Certain of these bodies, at first, possessed few if any medical members. But professional goals were at least given formal recognition and the procedures established were never entirely forgotten thereafter.

The inclination to accept a medical degree in lieu of other requirements was not surprising. The M.D. conveyed much prestige when awarded by European universities, and the early American medical colleges measured up to this tradition. Medical graduates, as noted, were the counterparts of European physicians. Men licensed only on the basis of apprenticeship and examinations, in contrast, still looked much like surgeon-apothecaries. Yet in at least the one case of

Massachusetts, the first examining body originally sought to extend its control over medical graduates as well as over those lacking degrees. With regard to the former, the licensing authority attempted during the 1780's to function much as would a state board today.

It so happened that the Massachusetts Medical Society, when chartered in 1781, was given the privilege of electing its own members and also the power to license practitioners. Regular examinations were held for the latter purpose. Within its area, this society therefore realized for a time the ideal of a college of physicians as Morgan had envisaged it for Philadelphia.

When the Harvard medical school was opened in 1783, however, the question arose as to whether it also should be granted licensing power. The Medical Society at first declined to approve certain men who had attained a Harvard medical degree, but an ensuing public examination was so impressive that opposition was abandoned. Thereafter either the Harvard diploma or approval by the society qualified a man for practice.[56]

The final aspect of professional developments that merits attention was the increase in medical publications that ensued after about 1790. Prior to the Revolution these had been limited to occasional pamphlets and to articles in general magazines or in European scientific journals. (The only general work on medicine written before 1790, Cotton Mather's *Angel,* had never been printed.) Military experience acquired during the Revolution, however, had led to the publication of certain useful manuals, such as those of Rush on hygiene, of James Tilton on army hospitals, and of John Jones on the treatment of wounds. And in 1778 Dr. William Brown, of the military service, published a *Pharmacopoeia* borrowed from Edinburgh.[57]

Finally, after the pioneer medical schools and societies were well under way, 1790–1820, more general writings began to appear. In 1808, for example, the Massachusetts Medical Society brought out a pharmacopoeia by James Jackson and John C. Warren—based again largely on that of Edinburgh; and in 1809 the same society approved James Thatcher's *American New Dispensary*. More significant were the cumulative papers and monographs of such writers as Currie, Webster, Hosack, and Rush. Worthy of mention also were the interpretations of eighteenth-century medicine presented by David Ramsay (1801) and by Samuel Miller (1803).

Yet today, accustomed as we are to a plethora of medical works, it is surprising how few professional leaders of that time rushed into print. Among the original four members of the Philadelphia faculty, for example, Morgan wrote little except on professional themes, while Shippen and Kuhn brought out nothing of significance. True, M.D. theses were published by their students; but, as will be noted elsewhere, most of these efforts served academic rather than scientific ends. Samuel Gross later declared that "not one in fifty" of the old theses indicated any ability on the part of the author.

Even abroad, of course, medical publications were far less numerous than they would become within another half century. But there was an old tradition of medical publication in great centers like London and Paris, where professional leaders were expected to prepare texts on technical subjects. Few Americans spared sufficient time from practice to do this, though one can observe the first attempts after 1790. Notable, in addition to the compilations in pharmacy, was the appearance of Rush's famous work on psychiatry (1812) and of John S. Dorsey's *Elements of Surgery: for the Use of Students* (1813). But not until after 1815 were texts brought out in such central fields as pathology and general practice.

No doubt the appearance of systematic American works was delayed by the availability of British publications. Medical writing was shifting to the vernacular by the later 1700's and it was all too easy just to depend on standard English texts. And even the first books printed in the United States were, in most cases, based largely on London or Edinburgh publications. Although the Revolution left a heritage of anti-British feeling in medical circles, primary dependence on the literature of the mother country was not seriously challenged until after 1820.[58]

A partial exception to this statement may be observed in the case of periodicals, which could accept contributions of a limited scope. Medical journals proper, with a few exceptions, had not been founded in Europe until after 1730. By mid-century several British journals were available to American authors; and after 1783 both professional and national developments inspired a desire to set up such publications in the United States.

The Cases and Observations of the Medical Society of New Haven County appeared as early as 1788; the Massachusetts Medical Society published a number of papers in 1790; and the *Transactions* of the Philadelphia College of Physicians began to be issued in 1793. But the first medical publication that was clearly a periodical was the *Medical Repository,* founded in New York City in 1797 under the editorship of Dr. Samuel L. Mitchill and others. Among the better-known journals that soon followed were the *Philadelphia Medical Museum,* founded by Dr. John Redman Coxe in 1804; Dr. David Hosack's *American Medical and Philosophical Register* in New York (1810); and the *Eclectic Repertory* in Philadelphia (1810). The last, changing its name to the *Journal of Foreign Medical Science,* was edited by Dr. John D. Godman and played a significant role in calling attention to French medical research after 1815.

Most of these publications survived for less than a decade. With the exception of the *Journal of Foreign Medical Science,* they were chiefly devoted to reports by American doctors on individual cases and treatments. In a day when medical training was still sought by those interested in science at large it is not strange that some natural history was also inserted. In several instances studies appeared which were based on real research and which now seem quite significant; notably John C. Otto's paper on hemophilia (*Medical Repository,* IV [1803]), and Richard Bayley's reports differentiating croup and diphtheria (same journal, XII [1809] and XIV [1811]). By and large, however, little serious research found its way into this literature.

The volumes of the *Philadelphia Medical Museum,* for example, contained accounts of yellow fever, of surgical cases, and of particular remedies. Thus Rush announced that consumption could be overcome by opium and an animal diet. Other contributions had such titles as "Watkin's case of a burn"; "Otto, on nitric acid in a chronic complaint"; "Horse-shoe found in the middle of a tree"; and—a truly native touch—"On the management of the scalped-head."[59]

Although one could easily ridicule such items, others doubtless had some practical value. And the journals, despite their limitations, may have stimulated subscribers to report cases or at least to read more extensively. In all probability the typical practitioner had read little up to that time and the slow pace of scientific advances may even have made such a habit seem unnecessary. The practice of most men had seldom changed after their formative years. Yet the scientific tempo was picking up after 1810, and young men with M.D.'s were more sophisticated and literate than had been the majority of their predecessors. To such men books and journals made an increasing appeal. No one foresaw, of course, to what a flood the first trickle of medical publications would eventually lead.

Not until 1812, with the founding of the *New England Journal of Medicine and Surgery* by J. C. Warren and others, did there appear a medical periodical which was destined to a long life. Renamed in 1828 the *Boston Medical and Surgical Journal,* it reverted a century later to "New England" and has been published continuously to the present time. In like manner the *Philadelphia Journal of Medical and Physical Science*—founded under the editorship of Nathaniel Chapman in 1820—changed its name to the *American Journal of the Medical Sciences* in 1828 and has carried on to the present day.[60]

The survival of these two distinguished periodicals after 1820 was itself evidence of changing times. Cities were becoming larger and wealthier than they had been in Morgan's day, physicians proper were more numerous, and the opportunities for conducting a journal successfully were consequently more promising. Of all this more must be said in an ensuing discussion.

The prevailing tone in American medical circles during the first two decades of the nineteenth century was an optimistic one. There were the usual comments that more had been achieved in science over the preceding hundred years than in all past centuries and—now and then—even a hint that there was little left for posterity to do in the medical line. Within the States, moreover, medical institutions were being established and a guild of real physicians was emerging.

Professional pride was intensified by patriotic emotions. Now that political independence had been won, physicians sensed an obligation to achieve medical independence as well: free institutions would serve art and science more effectively than could the outworn traditions of the Old World. Was not American medical practice already equal if not superior to the best that Europe could offer?

Such were the opinions of certain young physicians who, after formal training in Philadelphia or New York, found European schools less to their liking. So, also, thought some professional leaders. Dr. Chapman, in the first issue of his new journal, declared that none of the criticisms directed toward American culture at large could be applied to medicine. Native physicians, he admitted, might be less "erudite" than Europeans, but "in penetration, and in promptness of remedial resources . . . we are perhaps unrivaled." Not content with these claims, he concluded: "It may be safely said that in no country is medicine . . . better understood or more successfully practiced than in the United States." [61]

In retrospect such enthusiasm seems premature and we can understand the disillusionment that ensued during the next few decades. But, here again, one should recall the circumstances. Many a physician of the early 1800's could still recall the day when his country had not possessed a single hospital, medical school, or medical journal. Indeed, there had not even been a "country" in the usual sense. For such an observer progress was more than an ideal: it was an accomplished reality.

Notes

1. "History of the Medical Profession and Its Influence on Public Health in England," *Brit. Med. Almanac* (London, 1839), pp. 13 f.

2. On the Continental guilds during the 1700's see, e.g., J. H. Baas, *History of Medicine,* transl. by H. E. Handerson (New York, 1889), pp. 557 ff.

3. E.g., in Crabbe's "Village," *Works* (London, 1840), Vol. II, p. 85. Better known are the descriptions of general practitioners given in nineteenth-century novels, notably in George Eliot's *Middlemarch.*

4. See Charles Newman, *The Evolution of Medical Education in the Nineteenth Century* (London, 1957), chaps. 1–4.

5. The story of particular remedies and their transit to America is given in James Young and G. B. Griffenhagen, "Old English Patent Medicines in America," *Chemist and Druggist,* CLXVII (1957), 714–722.

6. Wesley, like the Rev. Cotton Mather before him, studied medicine in his spare time. He has been termed both "a dabler in medicine" and a founder of a health reform movement; W. J. Turrell, "Three Electrotherapists . . . ," *Annals of Med. Hist.,* III (1921), 361 ff. Contemporary opinion on the value of popular medical works is given in David Ramsay, *A Review of the Improvements . . . of Medicine in the XVIIIth Century* (Charleston, 1801), pp. 25 f.

7. Appended to his *Health, A Poem* (7th ed.; London, 1742), pp. 37–39. See also R. H. Shryock, "Public Relations of the Medical Profession . . . ," *Annals of Med. Hist.,* n.s., II (1930), 310 f.

8. W. B. Blanton, *Medicine in Virginia in the Seventeenth Century* (Richmond, 1930), pp. 80 ff.; J. M. Toner, *Contributions to the Annals of Medical Progress in the United States, Before and During the War of Independence* (Washington, 1874), p. 106.

9. Channing to G. C. Shattuck, Boston, April 20, 1811 (MSS., Mass. Hist. Soc.); and his *Introductory Lecture* (Boston, 1845), p. 27.

10. Quoted in R. H. Fitz, "Zabdiel Boylston, Inoculator," *Johns Hopkins Hosp. Bull.,* XXII (1911), 13.

11. These estimates, made by Toner in 1874 (note 8), are now usually cited; e.g., in Michael Kraus, *The Atlantic Civilization* (Ithaca, 1949), p. 192.

12. Albert Deutsch noted this in "The Sick Poor in Colonial Times," *Amer. Hist. Rev.*, XLVI (1941), 563.

13. Blanton, *op. cit.*, p. 80.

14. As in Cotton Mather's correspondence; e.g., his letter to J. Jurin, Boston, Sept. 22, 1724 (Royal Soc., MSS.).

15. E. E. Hume, "Spanish Colonial Medicine," *Bull. Med. Hist.*, II (1934), 223 f.; and the papers summarized by MM. Laignel-Lavastine and Fosseyeaux in "Le Xe Congres Internationale d'Histoire de la Médecine," *Bull, de la Soc. Française d'Hist. de la Méd.*, XXIX (1935), 314 ff. On Mexican professional developments see J. J. Izquierdo, "Notas de la Academia . . . ," *Gaceta Med. de Mexico*, LXXXVIII (1958), 521 ff.

16. Such contemporary opinion is expressed in R. V. Mohl, *Die Polizei-Wissenschaft Nach den Grundsätzen des Recht Staates* (Tübingen, 1833), Vol. I, p. 135; for historical perspective on the German view see G. Rosen, "The Fate of the Concept of Medical Police, 1780–1890," *Centaurus*, V (1957), 97–99.

17. W. R. Steiner, "The Rev. Gershow Bulkeley . . . ," *Johns Hopkins Hosp. Bull.*, XVII (1906), 48 ff.

18. *History of the Province of New York . . .* , (London, 1757), p. 212.

19. W. J. Bell, Jr., "Medical Practice in Colonial America," *Bull. Med. Hist.*, XXXI (1957), 447.

20. H. Woodhouse, "Colonial Medical Practice," *Ciba Symposia*, I (1940), 384 ff.

21. D. J. Boorstin, *The Americans: The Colonial Experience* (New York, 1958), pp. 230, 232.

22. See R. A. Kessel, "Price Discrimination in Medicine," *Jour. of Law and Economics*, I (1958), 23 f.

23. Quoted in F. B. Rogers, "Some Paradoxes of Modern Medicine," *Phila. Med.*, LV (1959), 623.

24. F. R. Packard, *History of Medicine in the United States* (New York, 1931), Vol. I, chap. 3.

25. A. Deutsch, *op. cit.*, p. 567.

26. O. T. Beall, Jr., and R. H. Shryock, *Cotton Mather: First Significant Figure in American Medicine* (Baltimore, 1954), pp. 16 f.

27. See, e.g., Franz May, *Unterricht für Krankenwater zum Gerbrauche öffentlicher Vorlesungen* (2d ed.; Mannheim, 1784), pp. 5 ff.

28. Muhlenberg's published diaries are interesting in this connection. On Eliot, see the biography just published by Dr. Herbert Thoms of Yale University.

29. "Currents and Cross-Currents in Medical Science" (1860) in collected essays of same title (Boston, 1861), pp. 5–8; and his memorandum appended to S. A. Green, "History of Medicine in Boston," in Justin Winsor (ed.), *Memorial History of Boston* (Boston, 1881), IV, 557 f. See also H. E. Sigerist, *Amerika und die Medizin* (Leipzig, 1933), p. 58; Boorstin, *op. cit.*, pp. 236 f.

30. W. Douglass, *A Summary of . . . the Present State of the British Settlements in North-America* (Boston, 1753), Vol. II, p. 351.

31. Morgan, *A Discourse upon the Institution of Medical Schools in America* (1765; reprinted Baltimore, 1937), pp. 23–27.

32. Presidential address, *Trans.*, New York State Med. Soc., I, 139.

33. *Medical Inquiries and Observations* (4th ed.; Philadelphia, 1815), Vol. I, p. 255.

34. W. J. Bell, Jr., "Philadelphia Medical Students in Europe, 1750–1800," *Penna. Mag. of Hist. and Biog.*, LXVII (1943), 20 ff.

35. On cultural developments in colonial cities after 1730, and especially in Philadelphia, see Carl and Jessica Bridenbaugh, *Rebels and Gentlemen . . .* (New York, 1942); and Carl Bridenbaugh, *Cities in Revolt . . .* (New York, 1955). The latter work presents, e.g., pp. 199–201, a quite favorable picture of the urban medical profession of 1740–1760.

36. See Kessel, *op. cit.*, pp. 25 f.

37. Kessel assumes (*ibid.*, 25 f.) that it all began with the advent of the A.M.A. in the 1840's.

38. W. S. Middleton, "The John Kearsleys," *Annals of Med. Hist.*, III (1921), 391 ff.

39. The standard authority is T. G. Morton and F. Woodbury, *History of the Pennsylvania Hospital* (Philadelphia, 1895); but see also F. R. Packard, *Some Account of the Pennsylvania Hospital* (Philadelphia, 1938). Cf. John Howard, *The State of Prisons . . . and an Account of Some Foreign Prisons and Hospitals* (4th ed.; London, 1792), pp. 84, 96, 119, etc.

40. R. J. Hunter, "Benjamin Franklin and the Rise of Free Treatment of the Poor by the Medical Profession of Philadelphia," *Bull. Med. Hist.*, XXX (1957), 142–144.

41. Thorough accounts of all the early medical schools are given in W. F. Norwood, *Medical Education in the United States before the Civil War* (Philadelphia, 1944).

42. R. K. Merton *et al.*, *The Student Physician* (Cambridge, Mass., 1957), p. 11.

43. Morgan, *op. cit.*, p. xvii.

44. The authority on this later epic is Alan M. Chesney, *The Johns Hopkins Hospital and the Johns Hopkins University School of Medicine* (2 vols.; Baltimore, 1943, 1958); for a brief interpretation see R. H. Shryock, *The Unique Influence of the Johns Hopkins University on American Medicine* (Copenhagen, 1953).

45. W. J. Bell, Jr., "John Morgan" (MS., 1958), chap. 5; also *op. cit.*, pp. 442 f.

46. A vivid account of this riot is given in J. J. Walsh, *History of Medicine in New York . . .* (New York, 1919). See also J. C. Ladenheim, "The Doctors' Mob of 1778," *Jour. Hist. of Med.*, V (1950), 23–43.

47. Bell, "John Redman . . . ," *Trans.* Phila. Coll. of Physicians, 4th ser., XXV (1957), 108.

48. Samuel Jackson, "On the Condition of Medicine in the United States . . . ," *Phila. Jour. of the Med. Sciences*, V (1822), 210 ff. Sigerist *op. cit.*, p. 98, viewed the appearance of drug stores as a gradual response to Morgan's influence.

49. See Brooke Hindle, *The Pursuit of Science in Revolutionary America, 1735–1789* (Chapel Hill, N.C., 1956), pp. 121 ff.

50. *Ibid.*, pp. 295 f.; also W. J. Bell, Jr., *Science and Humanity in Philadelphia* (thesis, Univ. of Penna., 1947), p. 205.

51. W. B. McDaniel II, "A Brief Sketch of the Rise of American Medical Societies," in F. Martí-Ibáñez (ed.), *History of American Medicine: A Symposium* (New York, 1958), pp. 133–141.

52. Rush to D. Hosack, June 20, 1812, in L. H. Butterfield (ed.), *Letters of Benjamin Rush* (Princeton, 1951), Vol. II, pp. 1141 f.

53. C. D. Leake, *Percival's Medical Ethics* (Baltimore, 1927), pp. 37–50, 92, etc.

54. E. J. Marsh, "An Outline History of the Medical Society of New Jersey to 1903," *Proceeds.* of the Society, LX (1942), 5.

55. Sigerist, *op. cit.*, pp. 61 f.

56. Josiah Bartlett, . . . *Progress of Medical Science in . . . Massachusetts* (Boston, 1810), pp. 15–25; H. R. Viets, *A Brief History of Medicine in Massachusetts* (Boston, 1930), pp. 120 ff.

57. Isobel Stevenson, "Medical Literature Produced During the War of Independence," *Ciba Symposia,* II (1940), 523–527; N. Shaftel, "The Evolution of American Medical Literature," in F. Martí-Ibáñez, *op. cit.*, 95–118; J. S. Billings, "Literature and Institutions," in *A Century of American Medicine* (Philadelphia, 1876), pp. 291–366.

58. As indicated in medical library holdings; e.g., W. G. Malin, "Sketch of the History of the Medical Library of the Pennsylvania Hospital," in *Catalogue* of the same (Philadelphia, 1829). On anti-British feeling, see J. Eckman, "Anglo-American Hostility in American Medical Literature of the Nineteenth Century," *Bull. Med. Hist.*, IX (1941), 31 ff.

59. All these items appeared in Vol. III (1807).

60. See E. B. Krumbhaar, "Early Days of the American Journal of the Medical Sciences," *Medical Life,* XXXVI (1929), 240 ff.; re the Boston Journal, see Viets, *op. cit.*, pp. 126 f.

61. Editorial in *Phila. Jour. Med. and Phys. Sciences,* I (1820), p. 9.

II

Medical Thought and Practice 1660–1820

MEDICAL science in any creative sense was nonexistent in the early English colonies. We are apt to take this fact for granted: how could it have been otherwise within a pioneer setting? Yet, for all our assumptions, the explanations are not quite self-evident. Medical works were published in the Spanish colonies within the first century of settlement; why not in the English as well? Perhaps the answer lies in the relative wealth of Mexico and Peru in the 1500's as compared, for example, with Massachusetts in the 1600's.

Contrasts within the Bay Province itself, however, may have had some bearing on the situation. The Wilderness Zion harbored clergymen of some ability at a time when its medical men were empirics at best. May not the quality of ministers have had an inverse relationship to that of their medical brethren—save when the latter themselves enjoyed clerical status? Giles Firmin wrote Governor Winthrop in 1639 that he was "Strongly sett upon to study divinitie; my studyes else must be lost, for physic is but a meene help." [1] This state of things, when medicine possessed relatively little prestige, persisted a long time in some areas; more than two centuries later outstanding Yale graduates were more likely to become ministers than physicians. One need not linger over the contrast beyond noting that, if the better minds bypassed physic, medical science probably suffered in consequence.

It would have been difficult to cultivate science on the frontier even if tradition had favored it. Settlements were indeed small, poor, and isolated, and practical matters seemed more urgent than did detached studies of natural phenomena. Conceivably, Europeans living temporarily in the colonies might have pursued investigations, but nothing significant of this sort occurred in the English provinces during the seventeenth century. Bishop Berkeley, sojourning in Rhode Island, thought of tar water; but this hardly proved the vast boon to medicine which he had anticipated.

Various observers reported what was novel in America. But some time elapsed before it occurred to colonists that they might contribute to scientific understanding. One of the first to pose the problem of native originality was the Rev. Cotton Mather of Boston. He explained to an English correspondent in 1712 that not much could be expected of mathematicians (and, by inference, of other scientists) in colonies which "are yett so much in their Infancy as ours are." [2] Mather's view was valid enough in 1712. But he doubtless would have been surprised could he have foreseen that this argument about "a new country" would still be employed a century or even two centuries after his time.

It is no doubt significant that Mather raised his question at all. One senses implications that regional pride was awakening and that more might be expected of the colonies in the future. Confronting the same problem three decades later (1743), Franklin declared that—the first pioneering now being past—sufficient leisure for cultural activities was finally at hand. That Franklin's insight was generally sound has been amply demonstrated by recent historians. Yet the particular theme of *scientific* achievements in this country, for a century or more after Franklin wrote, has remained the subject of divergent opinions.

By about 1800 some Americans claimed that science would soon be pursued as effectively in the United States as in any European land. But from the 1830's the opposite opinion was expressed by native as well as foreign observers. Among the latter, we need only recall de Tocqueville and Bryce. As for natives, consider Simon Newcomb's remark in 1876: that for fifty years after Franklin's death "our science was little more than a timid commentary on European science."[3] And a current study states flatly that "Franklin was wrong" in his expectations for the future of science in America.[4] In contrast, nevertheless, a number of able historians—including Hindle, Kraus, and Savelle—have presented relatively favorable interpretations of the native scientific record during the later eighteenth century. And others have viewed the next century in the same light.

The question of the relative merit of American science thus continues to haunt critics and historians. How far our preoccupation with this theme reflects objectivity and how far a subtle nationalism is difficult to say. Ideally, in Western thought, science is not evaluated from a national perspective. Thus we shall not ordinarily refer here to "American medical science" but rather to "medical science in America."

Even so, it will be difficult to avoid comparisons between Old World and New. Colonies can hardly be presented out of relation to mother lands. One can only exercise caution, remembering that such comments may be unfair or unrealistic: unfair, because a single country in North America is not to be equated with all of Western Europe; and unrealistic, in the sense that we are apt to project national perspectives back into the colonial era. From the eighteenth-century standpoint, American towns were more comparable to English provincial cities than to London. And viewed in these terms, as Bridenbaugh points out, the American record may be more creditable than first appears.

Most studies of science in the English colonies emphasize the decades after about 1720 or 1730. For the present purpose, the still earlier period cannot be ignored but may be treated with brevity. For there is no doubt, as implied, that the first medical science in this country was but a fragmentary projection of European science to a distant shore. How far, to begin with, were the first American-born generations aware of European medicine and of its latest developments?

The seventeenth century, one recalls, witnessed brilliant scientific achievements; and in no country was this more true than in the mother land of the English-Americans. This was the time of Newton and of Boyle, when scientists as well as theologians declared that nature displayed the wonders of God's handiwork. It was also the age of Harvey and of Sydenham in the medical sciences, when physic promised to keep pace with physics along the advancing front of natural philosophy.

Yet few colonists seem to have been interested in the striking developments under way in English science. Such men as Winthrop the younger, the Mathers, and James Logan were in close touch with English scientific thought and even with the Continental. Winthrop the younger practiced medicine, and a few men who had been trained abroad did likewise. In such cases there was considerable knowledge of European medical views and practices. It is also true that educated laymen, planters and merchants, as well as clergymen still read medical works in this period. But, with three or four exceptions, the number of such publications in early American libraries was not impressive.

The best evidence for participation in the thought of the day would have been medical writing. But here we draw almost a blank prior to 1720, except for more or less popular items in newspapers and almanacs and a few similar pamphlets.[5] Thacher's statement on smallpox (1677), for example, was borrowed from Sydenham; and Cotton Mather's on measles (1713), though sensible enough, was likewise intended for popular consumption. Of basic themes there is no record before the third decade of the eighteenth century. Here, again, one observes the contrast with Latin America, where a few works concerning such matters as the circulation of the blood or the classification of diseases appeared in the seventeenth century.[6]

Various American writers, it is true, reported on New World flora and fauna and were encouraged to do so by an avid interest among

European collectors. Reports on novel, overseas species stimulated taxonomic interests for more than three centuries after 1500, and this interest created in turn a continuing demand for the latest discoveries.

Associated with the search for new species in America was a quest for new drugs, either through direct observation or by borrowing from Indian lore. Despite their sense of superiority, Europeans and colonists alike were open-minded about Indian medicine and more than fifty items are said to have found their way from this source into the Western pharmacopoeia. There were, in a sense, American contributions, though their exact history is not always known. Plants enthused over by English colonists, such as tobacco, sarsaparilla, and seneca root eventually proved useless or turned out to be simple purgatives, expectorants, or emetics. The potentially more valuable drugs, notably coca, curare, and cinchona, happened to come from Latin-American areas.[7] The last-named, a genuine specific against malaria, reached the English colonies via Europe about the 1720's.

With regard to *medical* taxonomy—the identification and classification of diseases—a similar search might have been expected for new entities in America. But there is little evidence, in accounts of early colonial suffering, of attempts to identify disease entities as such. Careful descriptions of scientific value awaited the next century.

The explanation of this delay lay partly in social and professional circumstances, but also related to the prevailing tradition in medicine. A summary of this tradition must be interpolated here, if one is to understand later developments in medical thought. If the summary seems complex, not to say confusing, it can only be remarked that these qualities were characteristic of seventeenth-century medicine as we now see it.

In recalling the medical science of the 1600's one first thinks of the establishment of modern anatomy and the emerging interest in physiology. The latter field, as in Harvey's work on circulation or Santorio's research on the "invisible perspiration," reflected the same enthusiasm for observation, experiment, and measurement as was expressed in contemporary physics. Medieval speculation was to be abandoned and theoretical rationalism was to be replaced by a careful study of facts—the Baconian program.

Yet such a program could not be established at once in so complex a field as medicine. Occult notions, theological presuppositions, and speculation about the nature of disease persisted side by side with measurements and experiments. Even astrology remained respectable in medical circles until almost 1700, and long thereafter on a popular level.

Implicit in this confusion was an ancient controversy anent scientific logic. Baconians, in their reaction against the medieval heritage, demanded a strict empiricism and even viewed hypotheses as suspect; while "rationalists," in contrast, held that observation without reasoning was blind and indicted their opponents as "mere empirics." Sensible compromises were later suggested [8] but could not be implemented until experience had been gained with the limitations of speculative rationalism, on the one hand, and of rigid empiricism, on the other. That stage, unhappily, was not reached in medical science until the later nineteenth century.

Easily overlooked, moreover, is the fact that scientific advances in the 1600's had little bearing on medicine proper; that is, on the prevention or cure of disease. Anatomy was of value to surgeons, but otherwise it and the related physiology were of only tangential interest to most physicians. The latter, faced by the imperatives of current illness, found no help in the knowledge that the blood circulated or that the pancreas had a duct. The latest science did raise questions about pathology, as will be noted shortly, but provided no firm answers.

Basic for practitioners was the concept of the nature of disease. Most physicians, inheriting the Galenic and medieval views, thought that different patterns of illness were just variations in the state of the human "system." Striking "clinical pictures"—such as consumption, the great pox (syphilis), and the smallpox—had long been known and named. But therapy was directed against general body conditions, whether or not these were associated with particular names. In a word, doctors treated fevers, fluxes, and dropsies rather than particular diseases.

In the sixteenth century, however, a few medical thinkers had revived another Greek concept; namely, the view that different patterns of illness corresponded to distinct or "specific" diseases. Sydenham, in the next century, emphasized this so-called ontologic view and held that diseases were objective realities even as were plant and animal species. The philosophic background of this concept, as Professor Romenell has noted, may have been medieval realism—the doctrine of "substantial forms." But the immediate clue seems to have been the bedside observation that a given drug was effective against one clinical picture but not against another; ergo, two different diseases must be involved.[9] And such diseases, especially the infectious ones like smallpox, were thought of as entities which invaded men's bodies with dire consequences. We speak this language today in referring to "attacks" of one disease or another.

Those who held this view sought to identify diseases by their symptoms and then to classify them by similarities in what was termed a nosological (taxonomic) system. Although such a system might prove confusing, the ontologic concept did accomplish what theories about general states of the body could not do; that is, it encouraged differential observations of particular diseases. It opened up a vista of what we would call clinical research.

Whether physicians focused on general states or on distinct diseases, they also differed about what underlay the varied symptoms of illness. There was a natural desire to find some morbid condition common to all maladies, so that treatments could strike at the root of trouble and not just at its branches. But what was this underlying pathology or "proximate cause" of all illness? Since there was no verifiable evidence on the matter, theories were adopted in order to give some rational direction to therapy; and these theories appeared plausible if adapted to such scientific knowledge as was available.

The underlying condition of disease had long been viewed as a morbid state of the humors (blood, bile, and so on). These were said to be impure or out of place; or, again, were thought to be present in excessive or in deficient amounts. If excessive, the illness could be treated by depletion (bleeding, purging, sweating); if deficient, the patient could be aided by restoring the humors through diet and drugs. This humoral doctrine continued to be held by many practitioners throughout the eighteenth and into the nineteenth century.

Even before 1700, however, advances in chemistry and in physics led to new theories concerning the basic nature of disease. Iatrochemists began to think of illness in terms of the acidity or alkalinity of body fluids. Might not digestion, for example, be a chemical process and indigestion just chemistry "gone wrong"? Those holding such views, like the younger Winthrop in New England, were inclined to use mineral or other chemical remedies.[10]

At the same time the physics of Descartes and also of Newton encouraged the idea that physiology involved dynamics. Just as the heart was a pump, the stomach might prove to be a churn. Medicine could be viewed, ultimately, in the mathematical terms of matter and motion. More specifically, Haller's work on irritability and sensitivity in muscles and nerves attracted much attention, after 1750, to the nervous stimulation of muscles. Included under this heading was the possibility of nervous control of the muscular walls of blood vessels.

These ideas eventually proved to have some validity; but in the 1700's they set off much speculation about the role of the nervous and vascular systems in disease. Would not undue physical tension or a reverse laxity in these systems involve the whole body and thus serve as the proximate cause of most illness? This iatrophysical theory, with its corollaries concerning irritants, excitability, spasms, and the like, tended to replace humoralism during the later eighteenth century; and we will return to it when considering the particular views of Benjamin Rush and his British mentors.

Meantime empirical research on pathology also was under way during the seventeenth and eighteenth centuries. Anatomists, finding lesions in particular organs at autopsies, began to suspect that disease processes were really localized rather than diffused throughout the fluids or the nervous system. This view was long ignored or opposed by practicing physicians, however, on the ground that anatomists saw only gross appearances and could not detect from these the subtle, underlying conditions. As John Locke put it: "though we cut into the inside, we [still] see but the outside of things and make but a new superficies to stare at."[11] Although pathologic anatomy was thus easily dismissed at first, it continued to advance and was destined eventually to dominate medical thought.

Another empirical development was the dramatic discovery of animalculae ("germs") by early microscopists. It appeared that these minute organisms, by multiplying within the body, might prove to be remote or external causes of disease (etiology) as distinct from its internal or proximate causes (pathology). This concept was well known in the early 1700's.

In actual practice similar therapy was often used by the advocates of different pathologic theories—though in varying degrees. All were apt to employ *some* bleeding, purging, and sweating, and there was also much resort to polypharmacy. Remedies seem to have accumulated on a trial-and-error basis; but pharmacy, like pathology, also bore the imprint of ancient theories. By Galenic tradition vegetable drugs were considered most safe and effective. Then, from the time of Paracelsus, minerals (mercury, antimony) also were advocated. And there was, finally, much resort to animal concoctions. It is these biologicals which seem so bizarre to modern readers—lice, crabs' eyes, excreta, and so on—to say nothing of unicorns' horns and mosses adorning human skulls. The more rare or repulsive an item the more potent it appeared. Actually, though, our ancestors were "pikers" when it came to biologicals, in comparison with the present practice of injecting molds into human bodies on a wholesale scale.

To sum up, the medical thought of the seventeenth and eighteenth centuries involved unverified doctrines and resulting controversies. All this was, paradoxically, a sign of progress, since new theories were inspired by the latest discoveries. Science was stirring up medical thought and so overcoming the inertia of medieval tradition. Even the most dogmatic doctors abandoned appeals to classical authorities and claimed to be guided by experience. And means for advancing empirical research—which would call for further, theoretical adjustments—were becoming more apparent. Certain chemical or physical theses, unlike the humoral tradition, were potentially susceptible to verification, as was also the anatomic approach in pathology.

At the time, however, divergent theories exerted a divisive influence among physicians. This was especially true when men took extreme positions, presenting their views as doctrines on which there could be no compromise. And even if doctors differed only as a matter of emphasis the results could be confusing. This was often the case when they confronted such alternatives as those between rationalism and empiricism in method, between trusting nature and interfering with nature in therapy, or between the use of vegetable and of mineral drugs.

Physicians also differed in the emphasis placed upon various remote causes of illness, where they had a wide range of choice between supposed factors of a moral, an astrological, or a mundane nature. Only the latter category received much attention after 1720; but within it alone there were such varied possibilities as mental states, "airs and waters" (environmental factors), heredity, contagion by unknown poisons, and infection by animalculae.

The most complex issues, however, were those relating to the nature of disease. The doctor could choose between a theory of specific diseases and one which emphasized general conditions in the body. But in both of these cases he could view the underlying pathology in terms of the state either of the fluids or of the nervous and vascular systems. Or he could insist that disease processes were localized rather than diffuse. Anatomists might believe that such localized conditions (lesions) related to specific diseases, but it did not follow that all who preached specificity were convinced about localization.

Physicians today would see some truth and some error in both sides of these debates. Pathologists, for example, now employ generalized as well as specific concepts of disease, and consider both diffuse and localized conditions; while doctors, using chemical as well as biologic drugs, interfere with nature in some cases and not in others. The basic weakness in the old medical theories was the lurking "either-or" fallacy. It was easier and more impressive to take final, dogmatic positions than it was to discover how far one thesis was valid and how far another. Unfortunately, moreover, it was commonly assumed that *something* must be done for patients: if so, the doctor confronting illness could not suspend judgment until all the evidence was at hand.

So much for Western medical thought at the outset of the eighteenth century. But why analyze it here, one may ask, if isolated colonists were happily unaware of all this nonsense? The answer may be that men are moved by ideas as well as by motives of which they are not fully conscious. In any case the general background of medical thought after 1720 cannot be ignored. For in this later period American physicians were directly influenced by theoretical developments overseas. Hence their views are to be interpreted largely in relation to European origins.

During the century that lay between 1720 and 1820, two figures emerged as the most systematic writers on medical themes in this country. One, the Rev. Cotton Mather, wrote at the advent of this period; the other, Dr. Benjamin Rush, at its close. We may first consider how medicine was envisaged by Mather in the 1720's and later terminate the story by considering Rush's outlook in the early 1800's. In between there will be occasion to comment on the work of other Americans in particular fields.

The first general treatise on medicine written by an American was Mather's "Angel of Bethesda" (1724). The work nicely illustrates transatlantic contacts, since Mather drew on much of the medical literature of his day in either Latin or English versions. The study also illustrates most of the issues which were then current in European thought or which had been current in the author's youth. One wonders whether, since these matters were so assimilated in one American's thinking, they had not penetrated—if in lesser degree—into the minds of others? This surmise is more plausible because of the fact that Mather was one of the few Americans here considered who never lived abroad. Most of the sources and contacts he employed were available to any thoughtful Bostonian.

On the other hand, Mather's failure to find a publisher (no "angel" ever appeared to back "The Angel") does not suggest that *many* compatriots shared his medical interests. And the same failure prevented the work from exerting any known influence on later medical thought.

The "Angel of Bethesda" is unique among American works in providing a complex blend of medicine and theology. In that respect it reflected a clergyman's outlook and was reminiscent of the preceding century. Disease, Mather held, was ultimately caused by sin and was to be cured by prayer and forgiveness. But religious reasons were found for seeking scientific aid as well, and these opened the door to the author's obvious concern with medicine.

It is surprising, at first glance, to find that a minister who believed in witchcraft was meantime a mechanist in biologic philosophy. Writing in the Newtonian era, he viewed the human body as "a Divine Peece of Mechanism" and declared that medicine eventually would be envisaged in terms of matter and motion. Like European predecessors, however, Mather was unable to reconcile mechanism with purposeful behavior; hence he postulated a vital moving spirit in man and even a "Soul which animates the Brutal World."

In man the vital spirit was said to mediate between mind and body and such mediation explained the phenomena today termed psychosomatic. Bodily ills were caused by mental states, and vice versa. Parenthetically, Mather urged milder and more persuasive treatments for mental patients than did Rush more than seventy-five years later.

In basic pathology the clergyman assumed a humoral theory in commenting on certain cases. But he also harbored notions about a particular part as the original site of most illness. For Mather this was the stomach, or—as he put it in mechanistic terms—the "main wheel." The idea of tracing all pathology to a single organ or anatomic system long fascinated medical men. One finds it recurring often after Mather's time; as in Broussais's emphasis on gastroenteritis, in various neurologic theories, and in more recent osteopathic doctrine on the spine. The general concept, like that of humoralism, involves speculative oversimplification. It also represents localization of a sort but is not to be confused with the empirical localization of the anatomists.

Mather made no effort to identify diseases by observation but took for granted the existence of entities sufficiently distinct to justify diverse treatments. He showed little interest in bleeding but was much concerned with remedies. Most of the drugs he recommended were of vegetable or animal origin. Those he suggested were repulsive in some cases and credulous in others, but in these respects he was rather typical of his times.[12]

Although not original, the most distinctive aspect of Mather's thought was his etiology; that is, his acceptance of the animalcular hypothesis. He himself declared that "many" were familiar with the concept, and his colleague Benjamin Colman mentioned it in print. But Mather was apparently the only American to discuss this "germ theory" prior to the appearance of Dr. John Crawford's papers in Baltimore nearly a century thereafter. Assuming that minute "worms" were sent by God as the external causes of illness, the Bostonian immediately saw the possibilities of what we would call chemotherapy. Would not a safe but "potent Worm-killer . . ." he asked, "go further than any remedy yet found out, for the cure of many diseases"? [13]

Mather was by no means indifferent to preventive medicine, since he took a lively interest in public welfare. He suggested, for example, means for avoiding scurvy and occupational diseases. Indeed, his most useful medical contribution lay in this field: the prevention of serious cases of smallpox. The events associated with the introduction of inoculation at Boston in 1721 are too well known to bear repetition here.[14] But it may be emphasized again that Zabdiel Boylston, at Mather's instigation, inoculated some 240 persons with actual smallpox virus and that this was the first large-scale test of the sort in Western medicine.

Both Mather and Boylston demonstrated favorable results in statistical form. Mortality per cases in "the natural way" was shown to be about 15 per cent; by inoculation it was only 1 or 2 per cent. Iatromathematics was in the air abroad and measurements had already been used in physiology and demography, to say nothing of age-old employment in pharmacology. But the two New Englanders were pioneers in applying quantitative methods to what might be termed a clinical procedure.

Mather apparently associated inoculation with the animalcular hypothesis. In a letter of 1721 to Dr. John Woodward he remarked that it was "vehemently suspected that the Small-Pox may be more of an animalculated Business than we have been generally aware of." A similar statement was made in his pamphlet on smallpox, which was published in London during 1722 while the inoculation debate still raged. The clergyman did not say specifically that inoculation involved the injection of "invisible worms" (pathogenic organisms), but it is possible, in view of the statements above, that he had such an idea vaguely in mind.[15]

When confronted by bitter opposition to inoculation Mather revealed something of his attitude toward medical logic. Although he speculated on many matters, as revealed later in "The Angel," he proclaimed himself a pure empiricist on the smallpox issue. "Of what Significancy," he wrote, "are most of our Speculations? EXPERIENCE! EXPERIENCE! 'tis to THEE that the Matter must be referr'd after all; a few *Empirics* here, are worth all our Dogmatists."[16] He was not the first or the last to demand facts in principle, without hesitating to theorize when facts were not available.

The evidence submitted by Mather and Boylston encouraged certain English physicians in their support of inoculation, and Genevieve Miller has shown that such support never really declined after

1722.[17] Subsequently, despite its dangers, the practice spread from England to the Continent, and was meanwhile revived in the colonies when epidemics threatened.[18] Finally, Jenner's introduction of "vaccination" with cow-pox virus (1799) involved, from the present viewpoint, simply an improved form of inoculation. Hence the beginnings of preventive medicine in Western society can be traced back to 1721, and the part played therein by Mather and Boylston may be viewed as the chief medical contribution made by Americans prior to the nineteenth century.

During the era of Enlightenment which ensued after 1730 Western medical science became less credulous and more empirical in tone. The debate between empiricism and rationalism continued, for reasons noted, but astrology was discredited and theology faded out of the picture. Occult and repulsive remedies were gradually abandoned, and there was increasing demand for careful observation in all fields. These trends appeared almost simultaneously in Europe and in America.

A small but increasing number of medical articles were now published by American practitioners in English medical journals or in British and native periodicals of a general nature. Such papers commanded respect in Great Britain and occasionally appeared in translations in French or German. The record of such centers as New York, Philadelphia, and Charleston compared favorably, in this respect, with that of British provincial cities.

On the other hand, no notable discoveries were made by medical men in this country in either basic or applied science. In regard to the latter (that is, to therapy) it may be significant that the most striking contributions were made by the layman Benjamin Franklin. The greatest American *philosophe* apparently began his medical career by opposing inoculation in 1721 but later supported the practice.[19] He was subsequently on friendly terms with Cotton Mather and, like the latter, became well versed in current medicine without engaging in actual practice. Those of us who are over fifty can still testify to the usefulness of his invention of bifocal lenses (1785).

And his experiments with electrical treatments, though not of much help at the time except to quacks, had at least potential significance.[20]

In pharmacology B. S. Barton brought out a pioneer compilation of American plant drugs (1798); but neither he nor others found anything that was comparable, for example, to Withington's discovery of digitalis. Nor is the record more impressive in surgery, though this subject calls for further comment.

The surgery of the seventeenth and eighteenth centuries, although improved technically, was still largely a matter of structural emergencies—such as amputations, the excision of superficial growths, and the handling of fractures and dislocations. To some extent the anatomic knowledge, instruments, and techniques needed for major surgery were already available. But they were rarely employed to this end, partly because of the danger of infection. Another restraining influence, as Sigerist points out, was prevailing pathologic theory. Of what avail was surgery if illness resided in the humors: where was the man who could operate on the blood? As long as such views were maintained surgery had a place only on the periphery of practice.

In the colonies, moreover, surgery was in the hands of general practitioners who rarely had opportunity to develop special skills. Confronted by critical situations, these men occasionally "cut for stone" or patched a skull; and no doubt some of them were of great aid in such other emergencies as have been mentioned. But it is not surprising, under the circumstances, that nothing notable resulted from colonial experience.

During the French and Indian War and also during the Revolution military experience and contacts with French or British medical officers is said to have made for greater skill among American practitioners. This claim has been questioned, except perhaps in relation to wound surgery. A few men did become known for practice of this nature; for example, John Warren of Boston, whose surgical ability was highly esteemed by the 1770's. Generally speaking, however, little attention was given to surgery as such until almost the end of the century. Philip Syng Physick, who returned to Philadelphia in the early nineties, after training under John Hunter and with a license from the London College of Surgeons, is usually termed "the father of American surgery." And even Physick, who also possessed an Edinburgh M.D., engaged in some general practice.

Therapy and incidental surgery were the areas with which nearly all medical men were preoccupied. A few physicians became much interested in botanic taxonomy and in natural history, but the vision of what would now be termed "pure science" rarely appeared in the strictly medical field. True, it rarely appeared clearly to any eighteenth-century scientists, since little distinction was made between basic and applied studies until the next century. Yet the focus of American medical men upon immediately "useful knowledge," sought in studies of common diseases and their remedies, implies a relative indifference to biologic investigations.

Some interest was occasionally expressed, in principle, in more far-reaching studies, but little more than lip service seems to have been involved. In 1765, for example, John Morgan declared that simple observation in medicine was not enough—physicians "must dive into the bottom of things" by experiments.[21] What experiments, however, was not made clear. Again, as Hindle points out, Dr. James Potter of Connecticut urged his professional brethren in 1781 to "strain every nerve . . . and push your researches with relentless impetuosity through physics vast and ample field."[22] Such sweeping appeals, however, probably can be ascribed to revolutionary zeal: Potter wished to see medicine in this country placed immediately on a par with that in Europe.

More modest and seemingly more practical was a program to "advance the science of medicine" announced by the College of Physicians of Philadelphia in 1790. This statement was chiefly concerned with "diseases and remedies which are peculiar to this country."[23] The suggestion that Americans should focus on phenomena peculiar to their environment was logical enough: it had "paid off" in biologic taxonomy. The only difficulty lay in the premise that there *were* such native diseases even as there were native plant and animal species. The assumption was dubious and was rarely confirmed by later findings; hence, as a basis for a research program its possibilities were very limited. Here, again, perspectives may have been warped by patriotic fervor; one gets the impression that doctors took some pride in diseases "made in America."

The lack of medical research in the modern sense is evident in early doctoral theses. Many of these are library products of a semi-scholastic nature. Occasionally, however, one gets a glimpse of better things to come; as when Adam Seybert reported in a Philadelphia thesis of 1793 on actual experiments concerning the "Putrefaction of the Blood." It will also be recalled that the experiments of J. R. Young, one of Rush's students, demonstrated (1803) the acid nature of gastric digestion—following the work of Spallanzani and pointing in the direction which Beaumont would later follow.[24]

Let us summarize, in any case, the record of studies in such fields as anatomy, physiology, and epidemiology. Only in the last-named was much accomplished, presumably because it—of all basic areas—lay closest to practical interests. However, even the beginnings of concern with anatomy and physiology had some significance.

Colonial dissections and autopsies were not so rare as was once supposed. Before the 1730's, nevertheless, these were occasional incidents which pointed in no particular direction. The first formal lectures in anatomy, with demonstrations, were apparently those given by Thomas Cadwalader at Philadelphia in the decade noted.[25] Better known were those delivered by the younger Shippen some thirty years later, which were subsequently carried over into the first medical school. Shippen taught obstetrics as well as anatomy systematically and raised local standards, though neither he nor his colleagues are credited with original contributions in these fields.

With few exceptions, the record is similarly blank in physiology. Cadwalader Colden of New York, who sought to improve on Newtonian physics, wrote papers on "Vital Motion" and "The Animal Oeconomy" interpreted "Mechanically According to the Laws of Matter and Motion." But as the titles imply these were semi-speculative essays in the spirit of seventeenth-century iatromechanics. At the turn of the century came Young's experiments already noted. Finally, one Isaac Bull published in New York in 1808 *An Analytic View of the Animal Economy* which may be claimed as the first American text in physiology. This ninety-page work, however, was primarily a student manual—as was Rush's earlier text in chemistry.[26]

More original, meantime, had been the metabolic studies made by Dr. John Lining of Charleston as early as 1740. In a manner reminiscent of Santorio in the seventeenth century, Lining had measured his own intake and outgo over a long period and had sought to correlate resulting statistical data with those concerning seasonal weather and diseases. But one gathers that he was more hopeful of throwing light on remote causes or on cures of illness than on physiology as such.[27]

Lining's preoccupation with the weather, like that of Sydenham before him, was an indication of the growing popularity of the old "airs and waters" (environmental) theory of disease causation. Interest in the animalcular theory had now largely disappeared, for reasons which merit some attention in passing. This theory had been based on experience with large, pathogenic parasites and the revelation by microscopes of minute organisms which might play a similar role. Epidemiologic evidence suggested as much and lent the theory some plausibility, but laboratory verification was needed and could not be secured with the scopes and techniques then available. Even if techniques had been adequate, the identification of most infectious diseases was not yet specific enough to enable scientists to know what organisms they were looking for. A Pasteur would have found nothing had he searched for "germs" causing such vague conditions as "bilious fever" and "inflammation of the chest."

As Lining's work indicated, environmental factors in disease seemed a more promising field of study than did microorganisms. Especially significant, it was thought, was the condition of the atmosphere. This might take on a mystical "epidemic constitution," or, again, could cause illness directly through changes in the weather.

Popular opinion still supports the latter view, by the way, and it may have limited validity. But no one now takes medical climatology as seriously as it was considered in the mid-eighteenth century. Unfortunately, the general viewpoint may have inhibited public health activities. For if diseases came and went with the seasons or with other changes in atmospheric states, neither quarantine nor sanitation could provide much protection.[28]

Similar inhibitions on public hygiene could be expected of any theory which placed disease causation beyond man's reach. Another illustration was the growing tendency in Northern Europe and in the United States, by about 1800, to view consumption (pulmonary tuberculosis) as a hereditary condition. Short of some eugenics program, this meant that there was no way of preventing it; so that the disease was removed from the public health sphere just when it was becoming the greatest cause of death.[29]

The changing attitude toward consumption was more than an isolated phenomenon. It is true that certain other diseases were still viewed as contagious, and that isolation procedures inherited from Renaissance days were commonly applied during epidemics. But by 1800 an anticontagion trend was under way, since theories relating to heredity, to medical climatology, and to local miasmata all pointed in that direction.

So much for theories about the external causes of disease and their bearing on public hygiene. What, meantime, of pathology proper and of its implications for therapy? In the first place, Americans—like most Europeans—continued to ignore morbid anatomy at a time of striking advances in that field. The former Charlestonian, William C. Wells, was apparently the only American who pursued real research in this field. But since he did it after fleeing to London in 1783, it can hardly be considered a part of the American record. Wells was doubtless influenced by European developments, which must be recalled at this point.

In 1761 Morgagni of Padua published his classic work on the sites of diseases. Therein he demonstrated, more clearly than ever before, that disease processes were often localized. He showed, moreover, that by correlating lesions with ante-mortem symptoms more exact identifications of diseases could be made than was possible on a basis of symptoms alone. Here, one can now see, was a way out of the confusion of purely symptomatic nosologies.

Yet there is no evidence that American physicians paid much heed to Morgagni. He was rarely if ever cited between 1761 and 1800. Dr. Thomas Bond of Philadelphia did proclaim the values of morbid anatomy in a striking lecture (1766) but little was done to implement his views—perhaps because of the difficulties attending autopsies at that time and place. In any case, Bond did not discuss the Italian authority.[30] Dr. Rush possessed a copy of Morgagni's book, and Dr. Morgan visited the latter as a celebrity but showed no inclination to follow in his footsteps. The first, or at least the first well-known American tribute to Morgagni's work was that expressed by a New York clergyman, Samuel Miller, and his statement did not appear until 1803.[31]

While overlooking morbid anatomy in relation to disease identification, Americans did become more active in describing forms of illness in bedside terms. There were as yet no systematic hospital studies, and the examination of patients was superficial by later standards. But an observant man could paint a clinical picture if he saw many cases and if distinctive symptoms could be found.

Early colonial descriptions, as noted, had been fragmentary or obscure. Discriminating reports began to appear only in the 1730's and especially after 1750. Notable, for example, were those of Douglass on scarlet fever (1736), of Cadwalader on lead poisoning (1745), of Mitchell, Lining and others on yellow fever (1751 and later), of Colden on cancer (1751), and of Chalmers on tetanus (1757), on apoplexy, and on what was called peripneumony (1769). Such studies reflected a growing interest in specific entities as well as the European training of the men concerned.

In the case of at least one physician there was a parallel interest in the recognition of animal diseases. Few such entities seem to have been reported prior to 1750, but what was later termed Texas fever appeared at about that time. Dr. James Mease, port physician of Philadelphia, began in 1769 a thirty-year study of this disease, in the course of which he noted typical lesions and pointed out the role of immune carriers. In 1807 Dr. Rush called for general studies in veterinary medicine and noted the transmission of diseases from animals to men. And in 1813 Dr. Mease gave what were probably the first American lectures in this field.[32]

Although interested in disease identification, Americans rarely took the next step of attempting to classify their entities. Such attempts had begun in Europe as early as about 1600 and took on elaborate forms in the nosologies of de Sauvage, Cullen, and others in the later eighteenth century. In systems of that sort every supposed variation or combination of symptoms was solemnly named as a species of disease. What was apparently pulmonary tuberculosis, for example, was alone broken down into twenty different species. And on a basis of anywhere from one to two thousand such entities there was erected an imposing superstructure of orders, classes, and the like.

Certain American physicians who were distinguished as naturalists, such as Douglass, Colden, and Garden, were much interested in botanic taxonomy—classifications and all.[33] But, with the exception of David Hosack of New York, they either did not think classifications worth while in medicine or else viewed the European nosologies as adequate.

Meantime, most illnesses were still not clearly identified, either in an abstract manner or in diagnoses. Practitioners, unless extreme empiricists, continued to focus on general states—on fevers and fluxes—in terms of humoralism or of some other theoretical explanation. And since humoralism indicated bleeding or other depletion procedures, these treatments were undoubtedly used by the few physicians who were available in early colonial days.[34] It is difficult, as already implied, to say just how rank-and-file "doctors" practiced, but occasional comment on such men in large towns suggests that they also used traditional remedies.

Dr. Douglass, for example, declared that bleeding, blistering, and purging were widely employed at Boston in 1718.[35] Douglass, as a strict empiricist, did not approve these practices and was said to have persuaded others to modify or abandon them. As one critic put it, he depended entirely on "bare experience" and secured disciples who "being but half learned themselves, have not wit enough to discover the foibles . . . of their preceptor."[36] But just how these converts practiced thereafter is unclear. Not too reassuring is a report by Cotton Mather that the Boston guild, when confronted in 1724 by "that miserable distemper known as the griping of the guts," advised their patients to swallow leaden bullets. The theorist Mather, in condemning this remedy, displayed more common sense than did the empirics who prescribed it.[37]

No doubt this episode was an unusual one. And home-grown doctors who thought they followed common sense and experience may ordinarily have avoided extremes in practice. Much of the theoretical teaching of the eighteenth century, however, also indicated moderation of this sort.

Toward mid-century, as noted, the humoral pathology was partly replaced by theories about nervous and vascular tensions. The latter type of doctrine was advocated, for example, by such European authorities as Friedrich Hoffmann of Halle (1660–1742) and, in some degree, by Boerhaave of Leiden (1668–1738). Through their influence concepts of this sort migrated to Edinburgh, whence they were brought to the English colonies by returning medical students. Benjamin Rush later stated that Boerhaave's principles were long accepted in Philadelphia, presumably from about the 1730's until at least the 1770's.

Boerhaave was an eclectic thinker. His pathology involved both humoralism and nervous states and his practice was based on trust in nature in some conditions and not in others. He and his followers avoided extreme treatments in any case. Such was the therapy of Dr. John Redman, long Nestor of the Philadelphia profession, who reported that during the yellow fever epidemic of 1762 "practitioners mostly avoided venesection and emetics." He himself, during this emergency, relied simply on Glauber's salts and on a concoction of snakeroot.[38]

Later, when Cullen of Edinburgh placed more emphasis upon nervous tone than had Boerhaave, remedies supposed to stimulate or to relax this tone began to be used. John Morgan introduced Cullen's earlier teaching into Philadelphia in the 1760's. But even Morgan's practice remained relatively moderate, using astringents to strengthen tone or so-called emollients to lessen it as occasion demanded.[39]

One can hardly say, then, that pathologic theories necessarily made for heroic remedies. Some did and some did not. Insofar as Philadelphia practice was typical, Americans were fortunate during most of the eighteenth century in the treatments indicated by prevailing doctrines.

Only after Benjamin Rush formulated his final views during the 1790's were bleeding and purging given a theoretical impetus beyond that provided by traditional humoralism. Despite opposition, Rush and like-minded colleagues subsequently exercised wide influence—especially in the South and West—and their heroic practice became all too common during ensuing decades. In order to understand this changing emphasis in therapy after 1800 one must examine the principles on which it was based.

Outstanding among American systematizers after Mather was Dr. Benjamin Rush of Philadelphia. Rush not only exerted potent influence within the United States but also attained a greater foreign reputation than did any other American physician before or during his time. European historians may now have forgotten him but he remains a figure of recurrent interest in his own country.

A summary of Rush's many-sided career would be beyond the present purpose. Nor is there space to do justice to such particular phases of his scientific thought as his psychiatry. We must at once proceed, rather, to a consideration of his medical system. Recall only that as a student at Edinburgh Rush showed some interest in chemistry and in experimental physiology. But he was eventually most impressed by the pathologic theories of his teacher Cullen and of his fellow student John Brown.

Any reading of Cullen and of Brown makes it plain that Rush always "spoke their language." It is true that Brown broke with Cullen, and that Rush also disagreed with his teacher and made a point of denying that he merely followed Brown. Yet Rush's ideas are meaningful only if presented in relation to those of his Edinburgh colleagues.

Cullen had introduced his mature views, in 1774, by saying that theory was "dogmatical" and experience "empirical" and that both were imperfect. But he inclined to a rational approach, since there were more false facts than false doctrines and reasoning in any case was unavoidable. Among earlier pathologic theories, Cullen thought Boerhaave's respectable but Hoffmann's a great improvement, since the latter gave more emphasis to the role of nervous tone. Cullen declared that health and disease were primarily a matter of "the motions of the system"; that fever, especially, was "a spasm of the extreme arteries" induced by the state of the brain. Hence, this condition could be cured by that which would induce relaxation. The argument for this iatrophysical view related to the "constriction" symptoms observed in fevers (thirst, dry skin, thin urine, and so on), which were said to suggest the spasm noted. Cullen did not exclude humors from the picture but thought they were of minor significance.

Once a fever appeared, Cullen held, a state of debility ensued. Hence practice must be of a cautious nature. There should be no bleeding, for example, in the early stages of fever. Both bleeding and purging, nevertheless, were valuable means for reducing tension when used with discretion.

Cullen assumed the existence of disease entities and believed it essential to identify and classify them as far as possible. In order to do this he sought complete symptomatic pictures ("histories") and also viewed remote (external) causes as significant in making distinctions between diseases—a view later substantiated in the development of medical bacteriology. Moreover, unlike Sydenham and some of his followers, Cullen declared that morbid anatomy would in time provide some of the best clues to disease identifications. Although he did not exploit this approach, his analysis suggests how nosologic thought led into, or at least could be reconciled with, later research in pathology. So much for the opinions of the Edinburgh master.[40]

John Brown, meanwhile, had taken the concept of debility, which in Cullen was just "the first consequence of fever," and made it the basic disease state. Or, rather, he postulated two such states, one of direct (asthenic) and the other of indirect (sthenic) debility. The first resulted when remote causes or stimuli (heat, contagion, emotions) were too weak to balance the innate reaction ("excitability") of the body. In this case stimulants were needed in order to strengthen the stimuli. Conversely, if the latter were so strong as to exhaust the body, indirect debility ensued. And in that case opiates, cold, and depletion were indicated in order to lessen the stimuli.[41] Thus arose the Brunonian practice of providing "Scotch" or laudanum for many patients. One can understand the popularity of such prescriptions.

Rush, pondering the tenets of both Cullen and Brown, decided that debility was neither a consequence of disease nor disease itself. It was, rather, a predisposing *cause* of illness. The disease state itself always consisted of "morbid excitement." But since such excitement exhausted the body, his concept was close to Brown's idea of indirect debility. In a word, Rush reduced Brown's two states of disease to one.

Rush maintained, meanwhile, the pathologic doctrine of Hoffmann and of Cullen, namely, that the morbid excitement observed in fevers was "a spasm of the extreme arteries" or capillaries. As the Philadelphian put it, fever lies in an excessive, convulsive, or wrong action of these vessels. Also taken over from Cullen was the advocacy of bleeding and purging as effective means for relieving vascular tension.

Rush eventually carried his master's doctrine to extremes. Not only fevers but all types of illness were ascribed to capillary tension. Therefore, he informed his students, there was really "only one disease in the world."

Little evidence was offered in support of this sweeping conclusion. As far as fever was concerned, Rush noted the flushed skin which suggested distention of the vessels. And, since such "convulsive action" was observed in all fevers, he viewed it as the basic pathology of these conditions. Conversely, phenomena associated with some fevers but not with others—like various lesions—could not be essential to fevers as such. Hence morbid anatomy was of no great significance in medicine.

Rush would doubtless have held, for example, that intestinal lesions, viewed today as a basic condition in typhoid fever, were mere aftereffects of vascular tension, while we now view as secondary phenomena the very capillary reactions which Rush considered primary. The doctor had the cart before the horse here, but one can at least follow his reasoning.

Lacking much evidence, Rush sometimes offered farfetched analogies as if they were proofs. Thus, those who could not perceive a single condition beneath the appearance of distinct diseases were compared to those who could not detect the unity underlying ice, water, and steam. And he declared that the doctrine of one disease had done for medicine what a belief in one God had achieved in religion!

Rush exaggerated Cullen's practice as well as his doctrine. The former advocated, in extreme cases, the removal of as much as four fifths of all the blood in the body! Cullen had recognized the healing power of nature; but Rush, proud of his potent art, banished nature from the sickroom altogether. Best remembered in this connection are the extreme bleeding and purging he employed in the yellow fever epidemic of 1793. It was this practice which his enemy, William Cobbett, termed "one of those great discoveries which are made from time to time for the depopulation of the earth."[42]

What Rush most condemned in Cullen's teachings was nosology.

He saw in this only meaningless lists of names which confused practice. Valid as the criticism was at the time, Rush overlooked—for reasons noted—Cullen's point about disease identification on an anatomic basis. In this regard Rush also ignored Bond's early suggestions, to say nothing of contemporary research abroad.[43]

The truth is that Rush repudiated the ontologic concept in principle. There are no such things as disease entities, he held, so why search for them? The only reality, the only thing we can really see, is bodily reaction to adverse stimuli—to mental states within or to cold, miasmata, and the like without. He apparently never thought of animalculae as causal factors, by the way, though he did remark that insects seemed to be associated with the dangers of marsh effluvia.

It was these effluvia or miasmata, arising from decaying materials, which Rush held responsible for epidemics. Some medical climatologists still believed that such outbreaks resulted from an "epidemic constitution" of the atmosphere, against which little could be done by health regulations.[44] Rush also indicted the atmosphere, but now in the more definite terms of locally generated poisons—about which much could be done by proper sanitation.

Instead of the isolation advocated by contagionists, he demanded cleanups as both more effective and more humane. Although his anticontagionism was only partly valid, the doctor was forward looking in this context and may be viewed as a pioneer in the sanitary reform movement in this country.

Rush encountered violent opposition from contagionists during the epidemic of 1793, since the transmission of yellow fever was obscure and could be interpreted in terms of either miasmata or human contacts. Quarrels and debates ensued, along with a literature which represented more comprehensive studies of epidemiology than had previously appeared in this country. Notable were the writings of William Currie and of Noah Webster, as well as those of Rush himself.[45] In this as well as other respects, the Philadelphia upheaval over yellow fever reminds one of the smallpox drama in Boston some seventy years earlier.

Whatever can be said in praise of Rush's devotion to public health, however, must not divert us from the main theme of his medical theory and practice. Here his views seem reactionary rather than progressive. What a strange combination was his simultaneous advocacy, in 1793, of enlightened means for preventing disease and of sanguinary methods for curing it.

Rush's pathology became something of an anachronism even within his lifetime, inasmuch as "the Paris school" was actually demonstrating after 1800 the possibility of disease identification on a clinical-anatomic basis. But Rush, as noted, ignored evidence which did not suit his purpose. As Cabanis said in 1798 of systematizers in general, he first thought out his hypotheses and then just framed them with facts.[46]

During the first two decades of the nineteenth century, nevertheless, there was little open opposition in the United States to pathologic systems. Some physicians differed sharply with Rush concerning his particular views but did not object to theoretical formulations as such. Several other men, notably Dr. Samuel L. Mitchill and Dr. David Hosack of New York, thought out systems of their own.[47] If strict empiricists were still in practice they were rarely heard from: perhaps they were overawed by the faculties of the New York and Philadelphia schools.

At this point, however, two laymen expressed opinions on medicine which are worth recalling. One, the Rev. Samuel Miller of New York, provided in his *Brief Retrospect of the Eighteenth Century* (1803) a discerning account of the medicine of that era. Miller was critical of most systematizers except Rush, but he also granted their doctrines some merits.[48] It remained for Thomas Jefferson to condemn medical systems in principle. The Sage of Monticello had resided in Paris, knew Cabanis and other *philosophes,* and may have imbibed critical opinions from such sources. Be that as it may, he foreshadowed in a letter of 1807 something of the attitude which the Paris school would later arouse in the United States.

Jefferson recognized the values of anatomy and surgery but distrusted learned "medicine" because of its speculative doctrines and heroic practice. Referring to what he called "the adventurous physician," the Virginian declared:

> He establishes for his guide some fanciful theory . . . of mechanical powers, of chemical agency, of stimuli, of irritability . . . or some other ingenious dream, which lets him into all nature's secrets at short hand. On the principle which he thus assumes, he forms his table of nosology . . . and extends his curative treatment. . . . I have lived myself to see the desciples of Hoffman, Boerhaave, Stahl, Cullen, and Brown succeed one another like the shifting figures of a magic lantern. . . . The patient, treated on the fashionable theory, sometimes gets well in spite of the medicine.[49]

Logically, Jefferson should have added Rush to his list of theorists, but personal friendship may have interposed at this point. The two men corresponded amicably though they were at opposite poles in medical thought.

Neither Jefferson nor Samuel Miller, it may be added, yet envisaged the lines of progress which were then opening in Paris. Miller, as noted, recorded advances in morbid anatomy but saw no special significance therein. And Jefferson, in the letter quoted, made no direct reference to these advances. "The only sure foundations of medicine," he wrote, "are an intimate knowledge of the human body, and observations on the effects of medicinal substances on that." So far, so good. But then he added:

> . . . some diseases not yet understood may in time be transferred to the table of those known. But were I a physician, *I would rather leave the transfer to . . . accident,* than hasten it by guilty experiments on those who put their lives into my hands.[50]

Taken literally, this statement was conventional enough; but in context it seems to imply that Jefferson saw no other means for identifying diseases than experiments on patients. If so, he was as unaware of the promise of pathologic anatomy as was Rush himself. The President of the United States, valid as were his criticisms of "systems," apparently had nothing but traditional empiricism to offer in their place.

At Paris, in contrast, negative attacks on speculation were combined with a positive program of research. Diseases were to be identified along the general lines indicated by Morgagni. It was this program which was slowly but surely undermining Rush's position, even though he was unaware of the fact. The Philadelphian was, indeed, one of the last of the more speculative system-makers able to maintain a reputable status. He died, in 1813, still surrounded by an aura of professional distinction. In contrast, the German Hahnemann—whose homeopathic doctrines stemmed from the same era—lived long enough to see them thrust into the outer darkness of sectarianism.

Is there, in conclusion, anything more to be said on the medical principles of Benjamin Rush? Perhaps we should let his friend Jefferson have the last word in the matter. And yet, having recognized Rush's many limitations, one still has an uneasy feeling that a man so able and progressive in other respects would hardly have followed mere guesses or illusions in the major work of his career.

Let us, then, take one final look at Rush's system, this time from the standpoint of the present rather than from that of contemporaries. So viewed, surprisingly enough, it is not clear that the doctor's ideas were merely dangerous speculations. The essence of his theory, as stated, was the assumption of an underlying pattern of bodily reaction in disease—a pattern common to all types of illness regardless of the remote or external causes. This was just the opposite view from that which emphasized the external factors, such as specific disease entities. And here we are in the presence of basic alternatives, between which medical thinkers shifted back and forth both before and after 1800.[51]

Look ahead for a moment from the date of Rush's death. The Paris school of the early nineteenth century, as noted, focused on specific diseases. By the 1840's medical thought had swung from Rush's complete repudiation of specificity to an equally extreme affirmation of that principle—with the result that common, somatic responses were largely lost from sight. (The "either-or" fallacy persisted.) Then Virchow renewed the attack on ontology, again emphasizing bodily reactions—this time in terms of cellular pathology. Virchow, in turn, was overwhelmed after 1880 by a new ontology. This was inspired by bacteriology, which once more made specific diseases seem quite real and objective—incarnate, as it were, in pathogenic organisms. The latter view was taken for granted by recent generations, which may explain why we now find Rush's notion of the unity of disease so baffling.

Can we be sure, however, that we have yet heard the last word in the matter? Within the past two decades, indeed, the limitations of the specificity concept and the significance of bodily reactions have once again been brought to the fore.[52] Some potent drugs are now used not because they overcome the external causes of illness—be these microorganisms or otherwise—but because they modify the body's reactions to many if not to all kinds of injury. In a word, as Hans Selye of Montreal remarks, these drugs now serve much the same purpose as did bleeding in the 1700's.[53] Rush might have felt more at home in such practice in the 1950's than he would have in the medicine of the 1850's.

To suggest in another way how an element in Rush's thought still lives, one may quote two statements separated in time by some 150 years. About 1800 Rush declared:

> My view establishes the sameness of a pleurisy, whether it be excited by heat . . . or by the contagions of the smallpox . . . or by the miasmata of yellow fever.[54]

And about 1950 J. S. L. Browne of Montreal stated that

> . . . the symptoms of tuberculosis are the manifestations of injury inflicted by tubercle bacilli. But underlying them is the *general* response of the body to damage, *any damage*.[55]

Since Rush explained the "sameness" of pleurisy or of any clinical picture in terms of a common, underlying body response, the similarity to the current views of Browne and Selye is apparent. In both cases the role of external causes is recognized but attention is focused on the body's behavior: on what Rush called "morbid excitement" and on what moderns term "reaction to injury" or "to stress."

In the last analysis, then, Rush commands a certain respect as a medical thinker. Despite his indifference to research, despite his dogmatism, and even despite his sanguinary practice, he did grapple with basic problems and came up with a type of answer which—though one-sided—still merits attention. Like Mather before him, he borrowed widely from others but reached his own conclusions. In this respect both of these leaders place a stamp of some originality on early medicine in America.

Notes

1. Quoted in W. R. Steiner, "Dr. James Thatcher of Plymouth . . . ," *Bull. Med. Hist.*, I (1933), 157.

2. O. T. Beall, Jr., and R. H. Shryock, *Cotton Mather: First Significant Figure in American Medicine* (Baltimore, 1954), p. 65.

3. "Abstract Science in America, 1776–1876," *North Amer. Rev.*, CXXI (1876), 97; cited in M. Weinberg, "Science in America: Soldier of Fortune" (MS., 1958), p. 3.

4. *Ibid.*

5. Until recent years the Evans and Sabin bibliographies were the chief guides to minor or obscure medical publications. Now becoming available is

the microcard printing of all early American imprints, edited by C. K. Shipton and published by the American Antiquarian Society. Very useful for early American medical imprints (pre-1821) is the "Preliminary Check List" of the National Medical Library, 1958, to be published in 1960. A comprehensive listing of medical items in all types of English-colonial publications is being prepared by Dr. F. Guerra of the Historical Library, Yale University School of Medicine.

6. S. Jarcho, "Medicine in Sixteenth-Century New Spain . . . ," *Bull. Med. Hist.*, XXXI (1957), 425–441; J. T. Lanning, *Academic Culture in the Spanish Colonies* (New York, 1940), pp. 100 ff.; Juan Lastres, *El Pensamiento de William Harvey en la Medicina Peruana* (Lima, 1957), *passim.*

7. Historical studies are available for such major items as cinchona, coca, and tobacco. For a summary of the Indian story, see John Duffy, "Medicine and Medical Practices among Aboriginal American Indians," in F. Marti'-Ibañez (ed.), *History of American Medicine: A Symposium* (New York, 1958), pp. 15–33.

8. R. H. Shryock, *Development of Modern Medicine* (New York, 1947), pp. 67–71.

9. Knud Faber, "Thomas Sydenham, der Englische Hippocrates, u. die Krankheitsbegriffe der Renaissance," *Münchener Med. Wochenschrift,* No. 1 (1932), p. 29.

10. C. A. Browne, "Scientific Notes from the Books and Letters of John Winthrop, Jr., 1606–1676," *Isis,* XI (1928), 325; W. R. Steiner, "Governor John Winthrop, Jr., . . . as a Physician," *Connecticut Mag.,* XI (1907), 25–37.

11. D. Klemperer, "The Pathology of Morgagni and Virchow," *Bull. Med. Hist.,* XXXII (1958), 26; see also P. Romanel, "Locke and Sydenham," *ibid.,* 298 ff.

12. For statements re Mather see references in Beall and Shryock, *op. cit., passim.*

13. *Ibid.,* p. 90.

14. The most thorough accounts are in John Blake's papers; e.g., "The Inoculation Controversy in Boston, 1721–1722," *New England Quarterly,* XXV (1952), 489–506.

15. The letter to Woodward reappeared in "The Angel" (Beall and Shryock, *Cotton Mather . . .* , p. 161); on its history see T. J. Holmes, *Cotton Mather: A Bibliography* (Cambridge, Mass., 1940), Vol. I, p. 205; also pp. 11–13; and

Vol. III, p. 1201. See also Mather, *An Account of the Method and Success of Inoculating the Small-Pox . . .* (London, 1722), pp. 7 f.

16. *Ibid.*, p. 8.

17. *The Adoption of Inoculation for Smallpox in England and France* (Philadelphia, 1957), pp. 109 ff.

18. John Duffy, *Epidemics in Colonial America* (Baton Rouge, La., 1953), pp. 32–42.

19. Samuel Miller, in his *Brief Retrospect of the Eighteenth Century* (New York, 1803), states (Vol. I, p. 286, note a) that B. Franklin opposed inoculation in 1721. Miller cited, as authority on this point, "the Rev. Dr. Eliot." The latter may have been the Rev. John Eliot, who was corresponding secretary of the Mass. Hist. Soc. in 1809.

20. William Pepper, *The Medical Side of Benjamin Franklin* (Philadelphia, 1911), pp. 11 f., 28, etc.; C. Tourtourat, *Benjamin Franklin et la médecine à la fin du XVIIIe Siècle* (Paris, 1900).

21. *Discourse upon . . . Medical Schools in America* (Philadelphia, 1765; reprinted, Baltimore, 1947), p. 22.

22. Hindle, *The Pursuit of Science in Revolutionary America, 1735–1789* (Chapel Hill, 1956), p. 280.

23. *Charter . . . of the College* (Philadelphia, 1790), p. 3.

24. J. F. Fulton, *Physiology* (Clio Medica Series) (New York, 1931), p. 76. Young's thesis has been edited by W. C. Rose and published by the University of Illinois Press, 1959.

25. E. B. Krumbhaar, "Early History of Anatomy in the United States," *Annals of Med. Hist.*, IV (1922), 272; also his "Pathology in the British Colonies of North America," in E. A. Underwood (ed.), *Science, Medicine and History: Essays in Honor of Charles Singer* (London, 1953), Vol. II, pp. 135–140.

26. J. J. Izquierdo, "The First Book on Physiology . . . in the New World," *Bull. Med. Hist.*, V (1937), 73 ff.

27. Lining, to Dr. Jurin, Charleston, Jan. 22, 1740 (MSS., Royal Society, London).

28. E. H. Ackerknecht, "Typen der medizinischen Ausbildung im 19 Jahrhundert," *Schweizerischen Medizinischen Wochenschrift,* LXXXVII

(1957), 1361 ff. On present views re the weather see, e.g., R. J. Dubos, "Biologic Equilibria and Microbial Diseases," *Temple Univ. Med. Center Bull.*, IV, No. 3 (1958), 6.

29. R. H. Shryock, *The National Tuberculosis Association: 1904–1954* (New York, 1957), chap. 1.

30. "Dr. Thomas Bond's Essay on the Utility of Clinical Lectures," in T. G. Morton and F. Woodbury, *History of the Pennsylvania Hospital*, appendix (Philadelphia, 1897); reprinted and edited by C. Bridenbaugh, *Jour. of the Hist. of Med.*, II (1947), 10–19.

31. Miller, *op. cit.*, pp. 243 ff. On Miller see H. D. Piper, "Pennsylvania's First Historian," Univ. of Penna. *General Mag.*, LVI (1953), 34 ff.

32. J. F. Smithcors, "Animal Diseases in Colonial Medicine," *Bull. Med. Hist.*, XXXII (1958), 171–176.

33. Hindle, *op. cit.*, chap. 3.

34. But see the discussion of this point in Daniel J. Boorstin, *The Americans* (New York, 1958), pp. 213–216.

35. William Douglass, *A Summary of . . . the Present State of British Settlements in North America* (Boston, 1753), Vol. II, p. 352.

36. C. Bridenbaugh (ed.), *Gentleman's Progress* (Chapel Hill, N.C., 1948), pp. 116, 131.

37. Mather to John Woodward, Boston, Sept. 28, 1724 (MSS., Royal Soc., London).

38. Redman, *An Account of the Yellow Fever . . . of 1762*, Philadelphia, 1865 (1793), pp. 16–18. See also W. J. Bell, Jr., "John Redman . . . ," *Trans.*, College of Physicians of Philadelphia, 4th series, XXV (1957), 106 f.

39. Bell, "John Morgan" (MS., 1958), chap. 10.

40. Comments on Cullen are based on his "Lectures on the Practice of Physic," 1774 (MSS., Edinburgh College of Physicians), *passim*, as well as on his published works. The most thorough analysis of the theories of both Cullen and Brown is that in Ch. Daremberg, *Histoire des Sciences Médicales* (Paris, 1870), Vol. II, pp. 1102–1141; Rush is noted therein (p. 1141), as a disciple of Brown at one of the *extrémités du monde*. Re the professional focus on fevers at the time see L. S. King, *The Medical World of the Eighteenth Century* (Chicago, 1958), chap. 5.

41. John Brown, *Elements of Medicine* (Philadelphia, 1790), pp. 5, 20, 80, 140, 175, 183, etc. See also O. Temkin, "Comments on the German edition of Rush's Account of Yellow Fever," *Victor Robinson Memorial Volume* (New York, 1947), *passim.*

42. William Cobbett, in *The Rush Light* (New York, Feb. 28, 1800), p. 49.

43. Comments on Rush are based on the manuscript collections in Philadelphia libraries (notably those of the Library Company, the College of Physicians, and the University of Pennsylvania), as well as on his published works. Of obvious value is L. H. Butterfield (ed.), *Letters of Benjamin Rush* (2 vols.; Princeton, 1951). See also J. T. Rees, *Remarks on the Medical Theories of Brown, Cullen, [Erasmus] Darwin, and Rush* (thesis, 1805), *passim;* and, among recent papers, G. Corner (ed.), *Autobiography of Benjamin Rush* (Princeton, 1948), p. 364; Shryock, "Benjamin Rush from the Perspective of the Twentieth Century," *Trans.,* College of Physicians of Philadelphia, 4th series, XIV (1946), 113–120; and Temkin, *op. cit.*

44. See Benjamin Spector (ed.), *Noah Webster: Letters on Yellow Fever,* Supplements to the *Bull. Med. Hist.,* No. 9 (1947), 9; also A. S. Warthin, "Noah Webster as an Epidemiologist," *Bull. of the History of Med. Soc. of Chicago,* III, No. 2 (1923), 205 ff.

45. E.g., Webster, *A Brief History of Epidemic and Pestilential Diseases . . .* (Hartford, 1799).

46. P. J. G. Cabanis, *Du Degré de Certitude de la Médecine* (Paris, 1798), p. 97.

47. C. R. Hall, *A Scientist in the Early Republic: Samuel Latham Mitchill, 1764–1831* (New York, 1934), *passim.*

48. Miller, *op. cit.,* Vol. I, pp. 243 ff. Actually, the medical section of Samuel Miller's work was written by his brother, Dr. Edward Miller. See S. Miller, *Medical Works of Edward Miller* (New York, 1814), pp. 41, 61, 62 of included biographical sketch; also G. Chinard, "A Landmark in American Intellectual History," *Princeton Univ. Lib. Chron., XIV,* No. 2 (1953), pp. 55–71.

49. Jefferson to Caspar Wister, Washington, June 21, 1807, in T. J. Randolph (ed.), *Memoir . . . of Thomas Jefferson* (Charlottesville, 1829), Vol. IV, pp. 91–94.

50. *Ibid.,* p. 94. Italics inserted.

51. On the cyclical behavior of major concepts in medicine, see A. Villar, *A Propos de Doctrines Médicales . . .* (Paris, 1921), p. 171; E. H. Ackerknecht, "Recurrent Themes in Medical Thought," *Scientific Monthly,* LXIX, (1949), 80 ff.

52. See I. Galdston, "The Concept of the Specific in Medicine," *Trans.,* College of Physicians of Philadelphia, 4th series, IX (1941), 25–34.

53. Selye, *The Physiology and Pathology of Exposure to Stress* (Montreal, 1950), p. 784.

54. Quoted in Nathan Goodman, *Benjamin Rush . . .* (Philadelphia, 1934), p. 232.

55. Quoted in G. W. Gray, "Cortisone and A.C.T.H." *Scientific American* LXXI (1950), 35.

III

Health and Disease 1660–1820

IN 1793 Philadelphia, then the chief political, economic, and cultural center of the new nation, was visited by an epidemic of yellow fever. In the course of the summer and early fall nearly 10 per cent of the population died from this malady. If a similar mortality rate were to be reached in the summer of 1960, one disease alone would cause some 200,000 deaths in that city! What our reactions would be under such circumstances is difficult to imagine. But of one thing we can be sure: everyone would realize the significance of the public health.

Such realization, unfortunately, may come only with emergencies. Yet the state of public health is an ultimate test of the value of medical science as applied by the medical profession. It is also, of course, a test of many other things which influence community life —the physical environment, prevailing customs, and standards of living. Hence the history of health is more inclusive than is that of either medical science or the medical profession. What concerns us here is the outcome of all these circumstances in the record of a people's sufferings or, conversely, of their well-being.

In recalling the American story, consider first the Old World background of early settlers and the new environment which they encountered. The North American seaboard was located at such a distance from Europe that great dangers were involved in early settlements. The first English colony, it will be remembered, disappeared entirely even as had the medieval, Scandinavian settlements. Under these circumstances more men than women risked the Atlantic crossing and the resulting preponderance of males must have exerted a retarding influence on the initial growth of the American population.[1]

The Atlantic seaboard is said to lie in the "Temperate Zone," but its climate is obviously warmer in summer and colder in winter than is that of southern England. Particularly trying to Englishmen were the extremes, as in New England winters and in the semitropical heat of southern provinces. The latter lent itself to tropical infections and promoted the idea that white men could not work in the fields. That idea encouraged the importation of Africans, who in turn brought in African diseases.

European settlers, meantime, had introduced serious infections of their own. It is true that the most feared medieval scourges, leprosy and bubonic plague, did not carry over into the English colonies. The former had largely disappeared in England by 1600, but just why plague did not take passage in the 1660's is something of a mystery. If the disease ever reached the colonies, it was rare and of no consequence.

The pathogenic organisms which early settlers *did* bring over were, like their cattle, partially domesticated. Europeans had become accustomed to living with them up to a certain point—perhaps by virtue of the survival of the fittest among the hosts. Much the same thing may be said of Africans, who had long been exposed to most of the plagues which threatened Europeans. For some unknown reason, on the other hand, relatively few infectious diseases were indigenous to America. Hence the native Indians were exposed, as a so-called virgin population, to unfamiliar European plagues.

The results were catastrophic. Tribal groups were decimated or even wiped out by such diseases as smallpox, measles, and malaria—

an outcome which some early Puritan observers considered downright providential.[2] Such biologic warfare was usually unintentional but was doubtless more effective in "clearing the woods" for white settlement than were military operations.

One may sum up geographic origins by saying that the colonies served as a melting pot for diseases as well as for human populations. Europeans, Africans, and Indians engaged in a free exchange of their respective infections. And in the whole sinister process Indians were the greatest sufferers.

American fauna and flora connived in the spread of infections by providing appropriate insect vectors and the like. But native plants and animals proved, on the whole, to be resources for the maintenance of health as well as for other values. Supplementing European importations, they provided ample raw materials for food, clothing, and shelter. This became all the more true as technology improved during the eighteenth century; for example, when rotation of crops was introduced and, again, when the cotton gin was invented. Even the dearth of fresh foods in winter began to be overcome, at the end of the eighteenth century, by importations that came with improved communications.

Native plants and animals, as noted in discussing medical science, also provided native drugs. Colonists sought new remedies and had great faith in them. Even theology encouraged their assurance, on the ground that God would provide in each region medicines appropriate for its particular diseases. It is conceivable that one or two plants of medical value, discovered in colonial days, have since been forgotten.[3] But the fact remains that most "wonder drugs" of that era—and every era has them—were later abandoned or assigned to minor positions in the pharmacopoeia.

The faith in local remedies, effective against local conditions, raises again the question: Did the colonial environment present peculiarly American diseases? Or, to be more specific, did Americans confront illnesses not familiar to their European mentors? In the nineteenth century white settlers in Africa *were* threatened by strange infections, but the earlier migrants to America were more fortunate in the absence of diseases peculiar to native peoples.

Among the few entities first encountered by the English in America were several of African origin—in which category one can probably place hookworm infection, dengue, and yellow fever. Except for the latter, these were limited to the South, and even yellow fever retreated to that region after 1825. Malignant forms of malaria also appeared in that section, as well as the baffling "cachexia africana"—a disease of slaves which seems to have resulted from deficient plantation diets after 1800. Outside the semitropical states, one notes only the strange "milk sickness" of the Mississippi Valley. This serious disease, also reported after 1800, was eventually shown to be transmitted from cattle to men after the former had fed on poisonous plants indigenous to the region.[4]

Non-European diseases were interesting in themselves, but their number was not impressive when compared to the dismal list of those brought over by white settlers. The existence of these few exotics hardly demonstrated much need for a distinctive American medicine, though there was a limited justification for this view in the case of southern practitioners. The latter would, in due time, make the most of it.

Disease trends, apart from recurrent epidemics, are not easy to trace through the seventeenth and eighteenth centuries. Not only are statistics lacking for most of the period but it is also difficult at times to decide what entities were involved.

As far as infections were concerned, one can observe certain patterns which unfolded with increases in population and particularly with the growth of towns. Infections as well as deficiency diseases also were influenced, for better or for worse, by changes in customs and in standards of living. Before discussing particular diseases, therefore, it were well to consider the more general trends in relation to social circumstances.

The physical isolation of colonial farms or villages somewhat retarded the spread of infectious diseases. It doubtless took some time for hookworm to spread over the southern provinces. And an epidemic, burning itself out in a colonial town, would leave it free for some years thereafter, while the same disease might remain endemic in more crowded English communities.

Yet isolation never provided complete protection. In the first place, seaports were always threatened by imported contagion. Epidemics did spread from such centers to nearby towns, and smallpox found its way far into the interior via Indian populations. As the chief towns grew in size, moreover, they began to harbor infections in an endemic manner analogous to that of European centers. Tuberculosis, in the forms of both scrofula and "consumption," probably became more common in the cities. And even smallpox, ordinarily recurring at intervals, persisted for years at a time in Philadelphia after 1750.[5]

Early settlers hoped to find a salubrious environment. Experience had shown the dangers of low and marshy locations, but men were often misled by the good health of the first years or even of the first decades. After there had been time to contaminate water supplies, to infect innocent mosquitoes, and to create certain social conditions conducive to malaria, the fevers appeared as if from nowhere. Thus the Charlestonians of 1666 boasted that South Carolina was most healthy, even at "that time of year that is sickly in Virginia." Twenty years later, however, the proprietors were writing the governor that they were "very sorry for ye great Sickness you have been troubled with, which we Impute cheefly to the unhealthy scituation of Charles towne . . ." [6] Subsequently the city was actually moved across the harbor to what was deemed a safer location.

Herein one observes a pattern of early salubrity followed by serious fevers, which repeated itself sooner or later in most areas. New country always beckoned as a promised land, free of malaria, of enteritis, and—in a later period—of consumption. The quest for health as well as for fresh soils motivated continuing migrations,[7] but disillusionment usually ensued.

Although early fevers might be typhoid or dysentery, malaria was the common, long-run offender. For several generations after this disease was established, social developments tended to maintain or even to aggravate it. Factors encouraging the insect vectors (such as the provision of breeding places in cleared lands, millponds, and rice fields) were combined with conditions making for greater susceptibility within the human population (as when migration brought carriers together with nonimmunes). "Chills and fever" were the chief stigmata of expanding settlements throughout the eighteenth century.

All these circumstances, added to the existence of malignant forms of malaria in some sections, help to explain the high mortality usually reported among "newcomers" to any particular region. Good health was not expected among such folk until they had endured a so-called seasoning process, in the course of which those blessed with adequate resistance survived.

Only after a protracted period did reverse trends set in. As Ackerknecht has shown in his study of the Mississippi Valley, many factors were involved in the eventual decline of malaria—the slow reduction of breeding places by cultivation and drainage, the diversion of the insects' feeding grounds from men to cattle, and so on. It seems unlikely, in view of the persistence of malaria in some parts of the South to this day, that acquired "racial immunity" played much of a role. The first major evidence of a reverse trend was the practical disappearance of the disease in New England by the early 1800's; and it will be noted that this occurred before the introduction of quinine, of systematic screening, or of any scientific knowledge of controls.

Any discussion of malaria sooner or later involves a consideration of standards of living; housing, for example, was a factor in the incidence of that disease. Related to environment but less immediate in their influence on health, then, are the manners and customs of a people. These, in turn, are determined by cultural factors—as by religious tradition, folklore, occupations, and so on. Consider, for example, the customs of colonial Americans in relation to such hygienic categories as diet, clothing, bathing, ventilation, exercise, and sex.

English diet, which the colonists inherited, was reputedly a heavy one. In the seventeenth century it consisted largely of meat and cereals; but in the next century physicians began urging the use of greens and other vegetables. The keeper of the Chelsea botanic garden declared that, by 1750, five times as many vegetables were consumed in the London area as had been used there during the late 1600's. Beer, wine, sugar, and fruit also were introduced into the general diet.[8] But claims continued to be made that the English people overate and that nothing was more dangerous to health than their excessive appetites.[9]

Colonists, meantime, supplemented English with American foods. After the early period of settlement there certainly was an abundance; and among prosperous families hearty meals seem to have been the rule. Dr. Rush, recalling the middle-class diet of 1760, said that meat was served twice and even three times a day—along with wine, punch, and "table-beer." But Rush went on to say that there had been "a revolution in diet" during the half century between about 1760 and 1810. Meat, by the latter date, was being served only once a day and its place was taken in part by "a profusion of winter and summer vegetables."[10] Herein one apparently had the same shift in foods that had been reported from London some fifty years earlier. No doubt it reflected improved transportation between towns and rural areas, but some change in taste also was involved.

This change presumably benefited health in terms of what are now termed vitamins. The great difficulty in diets prior to the late eighteenth century had been the lack of fresh meats *or* vegetables during the winter months and the consequent threat of malnutrition. We now think of scurvy as an old maritime risk; who has not read of the "ravages of scurvy among the crew"? Hence we forget that it also appeared on land. It was at its worst in early settlements as a consequence of semistarvation but persisted to some extent thereafter. Cotton Mather, writing about 1725, declared that America as well as northern Europe was still "grievously infested" with scurvy.[11] There is also evidence that other malnutrition diseases were present at times in the colonies.

Well-informed persons were aware, even in the 1600's, that citrus fruits would prevent scurvy. They also realized the dangers of living on salt meats through the winter. But the rank and file of farmers were not so well informed, and fresh foods may have been beyond their reach in any case.

Even after what Rush called the revolution of 1760–1810, inadequate winter diets persisted among poor, rural people.[12] In the South, particularly, various circumstances combined to popularize the "hog and hominy" or "grease and grits" tradition later associated with deficiency disorders. And even if no specific illness appeared, malnutrition made for lowered resistance to infections.

Americans, it seems, have always taken water with their meals—a habit which Europeans tolerate only in the interest of international good will. In early settlements colonists contaminated water supplies, and many of the early fevers were probably typhoid or dysentery rather than malaria. Later, on farms and even in large towns, wells were depended upon and the dangers of contamination shrank to local limits. Not until steam-pumping systems were introduced, chiefly after 1800, were public water supplies provided. Then, by virtue of such "modern improvements," it became possible once more to supply typhoid fever directly to every home.

Spas were popular in Europe and the colonists soon discovered their own mineral springs. By the later 1700's a number of these—like "White Sulphur" in Virginia—had become popular resorts and have remained such ever since. Fashionable families "took the waters" inside and out and displayed some faith in their healing powers. The medicinal aspects of "water cures," however, were never as seriously heeded here as in Europe: social diversions tended to overshadow medical concern.[13]

Americans, to be sure, rarely limited themselves to water. The popular strong drink of New England was hard cider or "apple jack"; that of the upcountry from Pennsylvania south, "corn likker."

How devoted men were to the latter beverage is recalled by the famous "Whisky Rebellion" of the 1790's. The gentry, meanwhile, took their Portuguese wines seriously; and in the seaports both they and the general public were partial to rum. But gin does not seem to have made such inroads as it did in England.

Drinking was heavy by modern standards, among all classes and on both sides of the Atlantic. Drunkenness was often condemned in the 1600's and became so serious in the next century that London physicians secured laws to combat it. Similar measures were adopted in some of the colonies. Dr. Rush brought London attitudes to Philadelphia and became the first well-known temperance advocate in America. He believed that alcoholic consumption was declining by 1810. Rush also reported what he called "intoxication from opium," but there is no evidence that drug addiction was common at the time.

Except for the gentry, colonists depended largely on wool and leather for clothing. These materials were heavy and underclothing was uncommon. But after 1800, as cotton became available, washable flannels and muslins were introduced and made for greater cleanliness and comfort. Even styles improved from a hygienic standpoint, as tight dresses and stays were replaced by flowing "Empire" creations.

Personal cleanliness, of course, involved more than clothing. Bathing had apparently become a lost art in Europe after public baths acquired a bad reputation and were closed during the 1500's—probably in fear of syphilis. Few English cities had such baths as late as 1800. In rural America, moreover, winter bathing was just not feasible—imagine breaking the ice in "the old oaken bucket" and then heating the water over an open fire! T. J. Wertenbaker, writing of the colonies in the seventeenth century, stated that men and boys "went washing" in summer but that the practice was discouraged.[14]

When the first attempts were made to set up bathhouses in large towns there was some opposition on moral grounds. Thus, when it was proposed to open warm and cold baths at Philadelphia in

1761 "the religious societies" considered the plan "so unfriendly to morals" that they persuaded the provincial government to stop it.[15] Private bathing houses, nevertheless, became available by the next decade. About the end of the century a few families even installed home shower baths and the first tin-lined wooden bathtubs. How novel all this was is illustrated by a 1799 entry in the diary of a Quaker lady, who reported:

> Nancy came here this evening. She and self went into the Shower bath. I bore it better than I expected, not having been wett all over at once, for 28 years past.[16]

If such were the habits of well-to-do, city families, one need not elaborate on those of the rank and file. Nor is it surprising that scabies, or "the Itch," was a common affliction. More serious was the prevalence of body lice, which in turn led to typhus fever. This serious disease was not clearly recognized until about 1840, but it was a major cause of death in the immigrant ships and jails of the eighteenth century, that is, wherever the unwashed were crowded together in large numbers. The infection probably smoldered at times in city slums, where it was reported along with other diseases simply as "fever."

Living was not too comfortable in even the more substantial colonial dwellings. In winter water froze in bedroom pitchers and open fires gave very uneven heat. The common cold and acute respiratory diseases—pleurisy and pneumonia—were widespread. The great chimneys did provide ventilation, but all this changed as stoves came into use after 1800. Writing some decades later, Harriet Beecher Stowe declared:

> It is a terrible thing to reflect upon, that our Northern winters last . . . six long months, in which many families confine themselves to one room, of which every window-crack has been carefully caulked . . . where an air-tight stove keeps the atmosphere at a temperature between 80 and 90, and the inmates sitting there with all their winter clothes on, become enervated by the heat and

> by the poisoned air. . . . It is no wonder that the cold caught about the first week of December has by the first of March become a fixed consumption. . . . No wonder we hear of spring fever . . . and have thousands of nostrums for clearing the blood in the spring.[17]

Except in winter, farm folk—and particularly men and boys—secured more than enough outdoor exercise. By present standards, both men and women were often overworked. Hence there was little need or opportunity for outdoor games, and rural isolation did not encourage them in any case. It is not strange, in view of the circumstances, that English sports like football and cricket did not flourish in the American environment. There was some bowling and even a little football on village greens, but not until about 1800 was conscious concern displayed about the need for open-air games among city children.[18]

On the matter of sex relations, it is well known that early marriage was the rule and that birth rates per women of childbearing age approached a biologic maximum. Most peoples had some sort of contraceptive folklore but there are few references to this in colonial sources.[19] Religious opinion frowned upon it and the obvious need for population presumably added social pressures.

Frequent childbearing, combined with poor obstetrics, accounted for much of the ill-health and mortality among mothers.[20] Old tombstones sometimes suggest that women died earlier than men; as when one notes such a sequence of names as "Ezra: his wife, Faith, his wife, Hope, his wife, Charity."[21] But actual statistics, as will be noted, do not confirm this suspicion. Female mortality may have been higher than male during childbearing years, but if so the latter more than caught up at other age levels.

Venereal diseases appeared in the seaports at least by the mid-seventeenth century; and Cotton Mather, writing early in the 1700's, fulminated against the many who were so afflicted. Incidentally, although it is usually said that realistic attitudes prevailed in that century, Mather referred to syphilis as a "secret disease" and stated that it was reported in the bills of mortality "covertly under the

Term of a Consumption."[22] Venereal infections have always been associated with prostitution, however, and the latter was an urban phenomenon. It is therefore unlikely that these diseases were common in a predominantly rural population.

The particular ills suffered in the colonies are, as noted, often difficult to identify in modern terms. Interest in specific diseases was growing by the eighteenth century, but only the more obvious ones could be distinguished by the symptomatic criteria then available. How disentangle the various fits, fluxes, and fevers? When parish or municipal bills of mortality were published during the eighteenth century, moreover, many deaths were attributed to even vaguer categories: as to "old age," or "decay," or—most sinister of all—to "being found dead."

Best identified were entities with distinctive symptoms, such as measles, mumps, and smallpox. Most of these ills appeared in epidemic form, and the fear of such visitations was the most dramatic aspect of disease experience during the seventeenth and eighteenth centuries. Endemic ills, viewed as a part of the nature of things, might arouse only resignation or despair. But an unusual disease which spread rapidly seemed unnatural and could conceivably be prevented. Hence something should be done about it.

The first defense employed in early colonial days was, understandably, to beseech divine aid. There were calls for traditional fasts and prayers. These measures became less common, however, as secularism grew apace after 1750. By the 1790's, when yellow fever recurred in the seaports, religious appeals of a public nature were hardly heard amidst the clamor for medical protection.

Public reactions to any given disease, epidemic or otherwise, vary both with the nature of the illness and with the class of persons most affected. It was well recognized at the time that certain ills were more common among the poor, and vice versa. In a bit of Scottish doggerel a presumably humble person exclaimed:

> But save us from those maladies
> Thou sendest on the rich.

Sic heathen ills as grip and gout,
We dinna mind the itch.

Whatever the poor thought about it, diseases which afflicted the upper classes as much or more than they did the lower were liable to make the greatest commotion in society.[23]

A case in point was yellow fever, which not only attacked the gentry as well as others but was often reported to be more serious among whites than among Negroes. Conversely, certain entities which afflicted chiefly the lower orders, such as scurvy, scrofula, and scabies, aroused little concern. The same may be said of such causes of infant mortality as enteritis and "hives or croup," which were probably most deadly among the poor and which attracted little attention until the late 1700's.

In any given case, however, the nature of the illness must also be recalled. Yellow fever and diphtheria, it is true, were no respectors of persons, but it is also true that they were, in themselves, especially terrifying diseases. As for scrofula and scabies, they did afflict chiefly the poor, but they were also endemic and therefore were taken for granted. And in the case of gout one had a condition usually associated with the well-fed; yet it aroused no alarm—presumably because it also was taken for granted. In a word, it is often difficult to balance the nature of a disease against its class status in attempting to account for public reactions.

A further word may be said about the social psychology of the two most-feared diseases of the 1700's—smallpox and yellow fever. Not only were they epidemic but they struck suddenly, were relatively fatal, and exhibited revolting symptoms. Smallpox even left permanent scars which were a constant reminder of its dangers. Last but not least, there was good evidence that these afflictions might be escaped by running away, and mass flight undoubtedly contributed to public terror.

One has only to read accounts of smallpox at Boston in 1721 or of yellow fever at Philadelphia in 1793 in order to appreciate these circumstances. In the latter case, not only did business cease as thousands fled but local, state, and national governments all disintegrated. Even the founding fathers like Washington and Jefferson departed, and only the mayor and a volunteer committee remained to aid the victims and maintain order. Such was the public state of mind that Dr. Rush, meeting a child who suddenly smiled up at him, recalled that this was the first person who had so welcomed him in more than a month's time.

So startling was the epidemic of 1793 that it raised some doubts about the future of the Quaker City or of other large towns. Ebenezer Hazard wrote that the experience ought to check the "prevailing taste for enlarging Philadelphia, and crowding so many human beings together on so small a part of the earth." America, he added, should reject the "fashions of the Old World in building great cities."[24] This view, usually associated with Thomas Jefferson, may evoke a sympathetic response among modern readers, although the disasters now feared are more the man-made than the natural.

As has often been pointed out, however, endemic infections took a greater toll of lives than did the epidemic. The major killers, after early years of settlement, were the acute respiratory and intestinal infections—along with malaria and consumption.[25] The latter already seems to have been the chief cause of urban deaths by 1800.

The Philadelphia bills for 1807, for example, reported 306 deaths from consumption (not counting other forms of tuberculosis); while the nearest competitors were "cholera" (presumably cholera infantum), 189, and "convulsions," 127. As the city's population was then about 90,000, the total TB death rate must have been over 300 per 100,000—a figure approaching that for the later nineteenth century. Evidently the growth of cities in itself promoted this disease well before the onset of the industrial revolution.

Consumption was most widespread among the poor, but there were additional reasons for its failure to arouse any great agitation. It was feared as highly fatal, but since it was endemic, at this time chronic, and its lesions hidden, it produced no such terror as did the epidemics noted. In the next century it would even be viewed by the upper classes as rather fascinating—in a morbid sort of way.[26]

Likewise quite fatal were the same chronic, malignant, and degenerative diseases which afflict present society. Superficial cancers were recognized, but heart and vascular conditions, nephritis, and so on were hidden behind such terms as fits, dropsies, and decay. These illnesses most threatened the older-age levels and were correspondingly feared by elderly people—then as now.[27] But since the latter made up a relatively small part of the population, such diseases were not viewed as major problems.

During the late 1700's, judging by Philadelphia parish bills for the 1780's, about 50 per cent of all deaths occurred under the age of 10 years. The most dangerous decades in the life span were the first, the third, and the fourth—so far as total deaths were concerned. In other words, individuals who survived the tenth year had relatively good prospects until they reached the twenties, when tuberculosis and other respiratory diseases began to take their toll.

The history of particular diseases in early America can be traced only in the case of epidemic ills. This vital and often dramatic story has been told with care and need not be repeated here.[28] But it is appropriate to consider the efforts made to prevent or overcome illness, and to raise the question whether such efforts had any observable effect on disease trends or on the growth of population.

Much that was done in colonial society, both to prevent and to cure disease, was taken for granted. Settlers sought healthful locations; and individuals, in proportion to their foresight and opportunities, avoided extremes which were liable to lead to illness. Even the use of occult devices had the same end in view. We do not now think of witchcraft trials as public health measures but there was an element of that sort in them.

Medical practice was also carried on as a matter of course and was the chief means employed in dealing with serious illness. In giving tacit approval to apprentice training, as well as in providing laws about fees, provincial society recognized medical practice as an institution and adjusted it to the prevailing economy. But since medical science and the medical professions are discussed elsewhere, we need not linger over them here.

Of chief interest, in relation to the prevention of illness, were the more self-conscious efforts to protect both individuals and society. The most obvious way to check illness in a community is to prevent it in individuals. That will not be enough, since the whole is more than the sum of its parts. But something can be done by persuading individuals to live in as healthy a manner as the environment and the prevailing economy permit.

Rules about personal hygiene had circulated since medieval days, and their sensible nature contrasted sharply with dogmatic absurdities in medicine. But it was easy to give common-sense guidance about eating, drinking, sleeping, and the like; the real problem—then, as now—was to reach people with such literature and then persuade them to follow it.

The publication of European works on hygiene increased steadily with each century after the invention of printing: more such items issued from presses in the 1700's than in the two preceding centuries combined.[29] Such literature was, indeed, an important aspect of the Enlightenment. German authors, accustomed to paternalistic regimes, sought to enlighten rulers; and the latter in turn were urged to enforce hygienic precepts among their subjects. Even arrangements for recreation and courtship were to be regulated. But in France and England hygiene was a matter of voluntary instruction and was supposed to be consistent with the pursuit of life, liberty, and happiness.[30]

Notable in French and English publications was an interest in the hygiene of special groups: soldiers, sailors, slaves, and, last but not least, children. Early statistics had emphasized a common observation that the greatest loss of life occurred among the children of the poor. Hence, as humanitarians pondered the evils of English slums, the welfare of children attracted increasing attention. A foundling hospital as well as maternity wards and hospitals were set up in London between 1740 and 1750, and in one of the latter, between 1750 and 1789, infant mortality was brought down from 66 deaths per 1,000 births to only 13![31] This remarkable improvement resulted largely from better care under controlled conditions and showed what infant hygiene could accomplish.

Writing for the London Foundling Hospital in 1747, Dr. William Cadogan published an *Essay on Nursing* which was a forerunner of many other works on the care and feeding of infants. He demanded fresh air, fresh fruits and vegetables, clean linen, the abolition of swaddling clothes and, when possible, the discharge of wet nurses. Such writings did not reach the poor directly. But Cadogan's book went through ten editions between 1747 and 1772 and benefited all and sundry through the hospitals.

What was involved here was an informal program of education and it apparently brought results. Between 1750 and 1800 the infant mortality rate in England fell from about 437 per 1,000 births to only 240—a drop of almost 50 per cent in 50 years! In consequence, the crude death rate for the entire nation fell from about 36 per 1,000 in the 1730's to 27 per 1,000 in the 1790's.[32] Such a decline was unprecedented and it set off that increase in total population which so disturbed Malthus at the time.

It is clear enough that children were "discovered" in America also during the later eighteenth century. Life had been hard for them in the 1600's; and in New England at least their elders' teachings had made it even grimmer—if that was possible. Books written for children carried such titles as *War with the Devil* or *Spiritual Milk for Boston Babes*. But parental attitudes apparently began to relax by the 1740's and the devil was at least partly replaced in juvenile literature by our old friend Mother Goose.[33] Rising standards of living and growing secularism doubtless encouraged this trend.

In the changing social climate hygiene received increasing attention in America as in Europe. Now and then English publications were reprinted in the colonies, though some of the earlier items were as theological in tone as was Cotton Mather's medicine. Thus a work of the 1740's reprinted in Boston in 1761 opened cheerfully by reminding the reader that it was only through God's goodness "that we were not strangled in our Birth nor smothered in our Cradle." It was then argued that good health was helpful in preparing men for eternity.[34] But all this may be viewed as a theological introduction to a naturalistic hygiene.

By the later eighteenth century an entirely secular tone had permeated hygienic publications, as may be observed in Dr. Rush's treatise on the health of gentlemen. It must be admitted that with regard to children in particular there was no such obvious reform movement as stirred in England. Nor are there colonial statistics about declining infant mortality comparable to those in the mother country. It is hard to recall Americans who crusaded for child health. Yet one must remember that the evil circumstances which aroused a few English doctors, such as those in the London slums and workhouses, were not duplicated in American cities until after 1830.

That there was *some* American interest in child hygiene is indicated by the translation (1794) of Bernhard Faust's *Gesundheits-Katechismus: zum Gebrauche in den Schulen u. beym hauslicher Unterrichte*. There were also claims by that time of progress in child welfare. Dr. David Ramsay of Charleston noted "a great reformation" in infant mortality rates between 1750 and 1800. He said that mothers now knew how to care properly for the little ones, and he estimated that the average number of living children per family had advanced from 4–5 in colonial days to 7–8 by 1800.[35]

Fragmentary statistical data point in this same direction. Whereas figures quoted above indicated a 50 per cent mortality under age 10 in Philadelphia during 1782, the municipal bills for 1807 indicated that this ratio had declined to 39 per cent. The two figures are not strictly comparable, as the first is for one parish and the other for the entire city, but the contrast is at least consistent with Ramsay's claim.

No doubt the chief beneficiaries of better child care were the upper-class families. Hygiene, in most respects, was a matter of education and living standards. And when the first preventive medicine was offered in the form of smallpox inoculation poor families could not always afford the fees demanded. Inoculation, nevertheless, may have provided some protection to children on that level during epidemics.

What was true of inoculation was even more true of vaccination, when that much safer process was introduced after 1800. Yet vaccination was a voluntary matter, and here again there was probably some correlation between class status and protection against smallpox. Certainly the disease continued to cause many deaths after 1800. In Philadelphia between 1807 and 1817, for example, the annual number was never less than 30 and reached as high as 140. Indeed, smallpox remained a major cause of death in that city as late as 1861.[36]

Well before 1800, however, the advent of a truly preventive medicine and the disappearance of certain diseases had encouraged much optimism. Were not the most feared diseases—plague, leprosy, and smallpox—already yielding to science and civilization? Benjamin Franklin, like the French scholar Condorcet, even predicted that medicine would in time prolong human life indefinitely.[37]

The actual disease record, of course, hardly justified such optimism. Nor could Franklin foresee the recurrence of yellow fever just after his time. When this plague appeared, the authorities had long been accustomed to dual preventive measures—isolation and sanitation. The first of these was based on a belief in contagion; the second, on the doctrine that infections spread through the air. These views were not mutually exclusive as far as health in general was concerned, and authorities often "played safe" by implementing them simultaneously. But one theory might exclude the other in reference to any particular disease; and, in any case, one thesis was emphasized more than the other over long periods.

Prior to about 1790, with smallpox, throat distempers, and even plague in mind, Americans most feared contagion and therefore demanded isolation procedures. Provincial legislatures enacted quarantine laws for seaports; at first only when epidemics threatened but later on a permanent basis. By mid-century, in the larger ports, provincial health inspectors were appointed to examine incoming vessels; and in some cases a city physician was appointed to care for sick detained at so-called pesthouses. These men were the first "health officers" but they rarely held full-time posts.

Meantime, intercolonial or even intraprovincial land quarantines were set up between one town and another when epidemics occurred. And, within any community, families were restricted for long periods in infected dwellings—by armed guards if necessary.[38] In a word, isolation was taken seriously in emergencies but was usually applied in a sporadic manner.

The yellow fever epidemics of the 1790's brought demands in seaports for stricter enforcement of state quarantines. There was even some talk of shifting this function to Congress. Partly in order to improve quarantine administration, local health boards or commissions were established between 1793 and 1810 in most of the larger ports, and in 1797 Massachusetts adopted a law permitting any town to establish a permanent board.[39] Such bodies were also expected to report and eliminate local nuisances dangerous to health; and this objective, though rarely attained, reflected changing emphases.

Colonial towns, like European, had always given some heed to sanitation, as in trying to regulate objectionable trades and in providing for surface drainage. In respect to the latter they may even have been in advance of many European cities.[40] Nevertheless, conditions then taken for granted would seem offensive and perhaps dangerous today. They began to appear dangerous, at the time, just in proportion to the emphasis placed on air transmission of disease. This emphasis increased slowly after about 1750, on both sides of the Atlantic—perhaps because of some disillusionment about quarantines. Or it may be that the disappearance of plague and the advent of some control of smallpox lessened the fear of contagion in general. On the positive side, meantime, disease became more concentrated and obvious in large towns, and the very growth of these centers aroused some concern and a desire to put them in order.

About mid-century, both Cadwalader Colden in New York and Thomas Bond in Philadelphia demanded urban cleanups as protection against disease. There was some response; the latter city, for example, began to pave and clean its streets in 1762, and filled in its noisome Dock creek the following year. Bond was confident that further sanitary efforts would promote health and pay for themselves in the process through savings in medical bills.[41] The latter claim would be echoed by many a health reformer thereafter.

Between the 1760's and the nineties, however, no special sanitary programs were developed. Yet there was much to be desired along this line. Few European and no American cities yet possessed sewage systems. Waterworks existed in some large European centers; they had been available in London, for example, for some two centuries. In the colonies a private water company had operated temporarily in Boston as early as 1652; and the Moravians had set up water systems at Bethlehem, Pennsylvania, about 1755 and at Salem, North Carolina, by the 1780's. But, with these exceptions, all American towns of 1790 still depended simply on wells for water supplies.[42]

When yellow fever descended on American ports during the nineties, mass behavior indicated a persisting fear of contagion and there was much resentment against noncontagionists who blamed the disease on local conditions.[43] But informed opinion—as among physicians—was now seriously divided between those who ascribed yellow fever to imported contagion and those who related it to local filth and therefore advocated cleanup programs.

The immediate effect of the epidemics was a tightening of both port and inland quarantines but some impetus was also given to sanitary reform. Unfortunately, the latter process was more expensive than isolation procedures, so that progress was slow. The first advances were made in relation to water supplies, presumably because these promised much for convenience and fire protection as well as for public health. The availability of steam engines and other technical factors also encouraged plans for water systems.

New York, Boston, and Philadelphia established waterworks

about 1800; and so, likewise, did several smaller New England and New Jersey towns. Baltimore came into line by 1807. Only in Philadelphia was the water system a public one, though its example would eventually be followed in nearly all municipalities.[44]

The early water companies faced many technical and financial difficulties. Since they charged for their product, the poorer streets were slow in securing connections. And, as far as health values were concerned, problems arose concerning the safety of the water supplied. Meantime, in the absence of sewage systems, the general sanitary state of cities still left much to be desired. Thus Dr. Rush complained in 1809 that Philadelphia was full of stagnant pools, that the docks had not been cleaned in over thirty years, and that privies were exceedingly offensive.[45]

Whether the few sanitary advances made before 1820 actually benefited health is difficult to say. Presumably, when stagnant waters were drained or covered over, dangers from insect vectors were lessened. The relative freedom of large towns from malaria would seem to substantiate this. Whether water systems protected against enteric infections depended on the comparative safety of their sources and of the wells which they replaced. Filtration was suggested at New York as early as 1799; and filtering systems were actually provided in several Scottish towns during the first quarter of the nineteenth century. But, with one or two minor exceptions, no such action was taken in American cities until well after the Civil War.[46]

Whether or not the early waterworks offered protection against infections, they at least promoted cleanliness. What is more, the whole sanitary program encouraged the gradual development of permanent public health administration. This program was more complex than had been the old quarantine arrangements. In any case, the latter were continued, so that health administration involved both types of procedure by the early 1800's. Despite the rudimentary nature of sanitary controls over the next half century, it was no accident that permanent health boards and (eventually) full-time health officers evolved along with sanitary reform.

Despite the limited preventive efforts described, Americans—like other peoples—continued to view illness primarily as a misfortune to be met *after* it had occurred. Medical men were expected to restore health rather than to preserve it, yet even the former function can be viewed in a broad sense as part of a public health program. So, too, can those measures already discussed—such as the first licensing regulations—which were aimed at assuring the quality of the health restorers. And although "doctors" may rarely have thought of their services in terms of public welfare, there was a suggestion of this in the tradition of medical charity. The same note was sounded when practitioners were urged to "stay at their posts" during major epidemics.

Traditionally, however, Western society had not left such matters entirely to the medical guilds. Desiring some care even for the destitute, in the interest of self-protection as well as of humanitarianism, medieval and early modern cities had provided "town doctors" for this purpose. English colonial villages maintained the tradition, providing "board and keep" at a neighbor's home for the helpless (outdoor relief) and paying fees to a local practitioner who attended them. Since such service was a burden on local taxes, it was usually restricted to residents; and sick transients were often hustled out of town much as were tramps in a later day.[47]

Outdoor relief ceased to be practical when a town reached a certain size. At that point, again following English models, the destitute of all types were collected in a single institution. Thus Boston built its first almshouse in the 1680's and Philadelphia in the 1730's.

Indoor relief of this sort naturally involved much illness and infirmaries soon had to be set up. Practitioners, appointed to serve therein, continued to be paid just as they had been for outdoor care. The records of so large an institution as that in Philadelphia, during the late 1700's, suggest that a hospital in the modern sense was already beginning to take form within the almshouse. Subsequently this and other infirmaries attained a size which necessitated separate organization and they evolved into the first municipal hospitals.

The almshouses, meantime, were of no avail to outside patients. In an effort to care for this element, medical groups in large towns—beginning at Philadelphia in 1786—established dispensaries which provided drugs free of cost. These were modeled on an earlier one set up by the London College of Physicians, apparently as a flanking movement against apothecaries. No such motive obtained in American cities, where physicians sold their own drugs. But the dispensaries seem to have met a need and were in harmony with the humane instinct of the times. They subsequently evolved, in effect, into the outpatient departments of modern hospitals.

All the public services so far mentioned were envisaged in terms of charity and involved the stigma of pauperism. Although well-intentioned, moreover, they operated in a rather sporadic fashion and rarely met the needs of families which were poor but not destitute. Little was done, except at the discretion of practitioners, for "the medically indigent."

Perhaps the first effort made in this direction was the establishment of a Virginia state "insane asylum" at Williamsburg shortly before the Revolution—a pioneer institution which modern visitors in that community rarely see. But this asylum long remained a unique example not only of state care for "the insane" but also of public provision for a type of illness for which no person of ordinary means could meet the costs.

Mental disease was present in the colonies as in all societies. Every village had its "simple Simon," and violent "lunatics" were at first confined at home. Such arrangements, although brutal in some instances, had their merits insofar as home care might be preferable to institutional. Later, such cases were sent to jails or almshouses—the worst possible solution. The only instance of care in a medical institution, prior to the founding of the Virginia asylum, had been the provision of some rooms at the Pennsylvania Hospital in the 1750's.

Mental illness, of course, was unusual in both medical and custodial costs. Few if any observers saw in it an extreme case of the larger problem of medical indigency. Yet this problem had begun to worry farsighted reformers of the eighteenth century. These men were motivated by both humane feeling and a dawning realization that widespread illness weakened society as a whole. Various schemes were therefore proposed, in England and in France, for some sort of state health system which would assure medical care for the masses on a noncharitable basis.[48]

The first application of such ideas was made possible by the concomitant development of the principles of insurance. English towns, providing local medical relief under the Poor Law system, resented expenses thrust on them by transient laborers. Parliament was therefore persuaded, during the 1750's, to require that coal heavers on the Thames make prepayments to a fund which would meet their costs in case of illness. With this example in view, reformers urged by the late 1700's that compulsory health insurance should be required of all workers throughout the country.[49] Similar ideas were advocated in the Revolutionary assemblies at Paris during the 1790's and apparently would have been applied had it not been for military emergencies.[50]

Americans were aware of these developments but do not seem to have taken much interest in their larger aspects. Indifference may have reflected the fact that poverty was a less acute problem in this country than it was in European societies. The only large class which obviously could not meet medical costs was that of slaves, and this group possessed limited social security in the very nature of slavery. Although many Negroes received medical attention only from overseers or from masters, the owners of large plantations often contracted with medical men to care for all their "servants."

One or two states did experiment after 1783 with insurance schemes for the largest group of transient workers, sailors. And in 1799 Congress set up the Marine Hospital Service, under which all men in the merchant marine were required to take out health insurance. But another century would ensue before the application of this principle to the entire population would be debated in the United States.

Meantime, in Europe, men of modest means had long sought to meet medical costs through their own efforts. Various "friendly" or "beneficial" societies, *Krankenkassen,* and the like, collected dues or premiums from members and then met their medical bills when necessary. By 1800 such societies were numerous and had accumulated considerable capital. Eventually they would serve as a nucleus in the evolution of state health insurance systems. But here again there was no parallel development in the States, though fraternal bodies and societies which aided immigrants doubtless provided occasional help in times of illness. Only in the case of such families as engaged "doctors" on an annual, contract basis does any prepayment for medical care seem to have been maintained in the English colonies and the United States.[51]

In reviewing the circumstances of health in early America one almost wonders that so many people survived and that the country grew and prospered. There is, of course, a certain danger in focusing on disease and on its treatment or prevention. To the angels in heaven above the most important news from the colonies was doubtless the fact that large numbers were feeling well at any given time. This same note was occasionally sounded here below, as when observers declared that few doctors were needed in this area or that. Even present historians have remarked on the good health of certain communities.

On the other hand, "good health" in such a context is a relative matter. What was good from the contemporary viewpoint might not seem so happy a state today. In order to gain a comparative perspective one may turn to the vital statistics. These exist, apart from some local data, only for the late eighteenth century and ensuing periods. They are, moreover, fragmentary and none too reliable. Yet they are the best guide available for an over-all assessment of health in early America.

It is a truism that both birth and death rates were relatively high in this country, as elsewhere, during the eighteenth century. Burial records for Boston, late in that era, indicated an average annual mortality of 33 per 1,000 whites and of 70 per 1,000 Negroes. (The corresponding figures for the United States in 1945 were, respectively, 10.5 and 12.) The population, in consequence, was heavily weighted by the lower-age group; near the end of the period noted (1789), the majority of white males in the United States were under 16 years of age. The high mortality among children and young adults, moreover, made for a low life expectancy at birth; and the latter figure is usually the most significant index of a people's health.

No doubt circumstances varied from one area to another. But the average life expectancy in some sixty Massachusetts and New Hampshire "towns" in 1789, according to the contemporary tables, was only 34.5 years for males and two years longer for females. Parenthetically, the cosmic injustice of this sex discrepancy has persisted into our own times and has never been adequately explained.

In any case, these are the sort of figures which were expected a decade or two ago in so-called underdeveloped countries. Anyone familiar with recent health conditions in such lands can picture those which obtained in this country as late as 1800. By way of comparison, it will be recalled that present expectancy at birth in the United States is close to 68 even among males.

Individuals who survived until 10 or 20 years old, in the Massachusetts of 1789, enjoyed a marked extension in expectancy. At the latter age both sexes could look forward to about 34 more years of life. Hence the average man at 20 could expect to live until 54, the average woman until 56.

At age 20 the contrast with recent figures was not so marked as it was for expectancy at birth. In 1945, for example, the average expectancy at 20 for all males in the United States was about 49 years; for females, 53. But this meant that males at that age could expect to survive on the average until 69, females to 73. Hence there was still a difference of 15 years or more, even on this level, between life prospects in New England in 1789 and those in the United States as a whole in 1945. And that gap has widened over the past fifteen years.[52]

Men may differ on moral or religious grounds, of course, about the desirability of extending the average life span under all circumstances. Although this objective has usually been taken for granted in public health work, some thoughtful critics of recent decades have expressed serious doubts about it. They are concerned about the increase in chronic illness which mass survival into old age is liable to entail.[53]

The urgent need in all countries at the end of the eighteenth century, however, was just the reverse: How to extend life expectancy by lessening acute illness during early years? There were a few who questioned this effort for fear of resulting overpopulation—a problem which has returned to haunt us in reference to underdeveloped countries today. But that issue had no relevance for the underpopulated United States; and, in any case, most thinkers agreed that the slaughter of the innocents must be stopped if possible.

For all practical purposes, therefore, we may assume that an extension of life expectancy was the summum bonum of health programs in the late eighteenth century. And, in terms of this goal, health conditions in Massachusetts were very bad by modern standards. They were probably worse in some of the other states. The picture of much ill-health which emerges from any survey of that period is therefore not so overdrawn as might first appear.

Yet, admitting all this, there were other points of reference which cannot be ignored in any final analysis. The first of these was the historical perspective available to the observer of the 1790's. Without benefit of statistics, one cannot say positively that life expectancy in that decade was longer than it had been in 1700 or even in 1650. Wertenbaker cites figures for life expectancy at 20, in a seventeenth-century Massachusetts village, which were higher than those noted above for that state as a whole in 1789.[54] How complete the data for the earlier computation were, however, is not clear. And in any case one would have to determine expectancy at birth in order to see the seventeenth-century picture as a whole. So we are still left in some uncertainty about the long-run trend.

The history of population growth is of little help in this connection, since it is influenced by other variables besides mortality. Not only immigration but also an increase in the ratio of women to total numbers made for population expansion, even if both the birth rate (per given number of women) and mortality remained constants. Something of this sort probably did occur in certain places and periods.

On the other hand, we know that standards of living rose during the eighteenth century, and this phenomenon is usually associated with declining death rates and increasing life expectancy. We also know, more specifically, that mortality from one major disease (malaria) fell as communities matured and living became more comfortable. This trend was already well advanced in New England by the 1790's. Tuberculosis, along with the crude death rate, may already have been moving in the reverse direction in large towns, but the latter made up a very small part of the total population.

Finally, as noted, there were hints that infant mortality was falling by the late 1700's. Cotton Mather, appalled in 1724 by the tragedy of the little ones, could only exclaim helplessly: "O how unsearchable the Judgements of God, and His Ways past finding out. The lamps but just litt up, and blown out again." [55] But Ramsay, by 1800, at least claimed that an increasing proportion of children was surviving and credited this to more sensible hygiene.

It seems possible, then, that American health conditions improved slightly during the second half of the eighteenth century. Such progress, assuming that it did occur, was slow, but it may have accounted in part for the medical optimism of that era.

Theoretically, a third perspective on American health conditions in 1800 was afforded by comparisons in space rather than in time. No attempt is made here to contrast life expectancy estimates of

1790 for European countries and for the United States. The data needed for such a venture, insofar as they exist, are obscure and fragmentary. One notes, for example, that expectancy in Massachusetts at age 20 in 1789 (34 years) was better than the corresponding figure for London, 1790–1799 (28 years); [56] but the average for all England was doubtless higher than that for the metropolis. Moreover, even if the national figure for Old England were shown to be below that for the New England state, it would not necessarily follow that it was lower than that for the United States as a whole.

One may therefore picture this country, at the advent of the nineteenth century, as sharing somewhat in the improvement in child health which was typical of progressive Western lands at that time. After having experienced the most extreme dangers from disease in some of the early settlements, American society had gone a long way by 1800 toward achieving at least a parity with advanced European nations in its health record.

Indeed, although it cannot be demonstrated statistically, it seems likely that Americans enjoyed some advantages in this respect. Except for vaccination, improvements in health could be largely credited to conscious hygiene and to rising living standards; and insofar as these standards were already higher among American farmers than among European peasants or proletarians, the former probably benefited accordingly. Moreover, this country had only just begun to encounter the dangers inherent in large cities, such as those long experienced in teeming European centers like London and Paris.

Ironically enough, the only risks peculiar to the United States in 1800—apart from diseases unknown in Europe—were those involved in an especially heroic type of medical practice. Extreme bleeding and purging, though based on ideas imported from Scotland, flourished in this country as they rarely did at the time abroad. When American "doctors" first arrived with their lancets and pills in New Orleans after 1803, they and all their wicked works were promptly opposed by the established French practitioners.[57] The contrast, implicit in this little drama, had real significance for public health. But no one will ever know just what impact heroic practice had on American vital statistics: therapy was never listed among the causes of death.

Notes

1. Wyndham Blanton and Carl Bridenbaugh have both called attention recently to this factor; see the former's "Epidemics, Real and Imaginary, and Other Factors Influencing Seventeenth Century Virginia's Population," *Bull. Med. Hist.*, XXXI (1957), 454–462.

2. See, e.g., Cotton Mather, *Magnalia Christi Americana* (Hartford, 1855), Vol. I, p. 51. General accounts of Indian mortality are given in P. M. Ashburn, *The Ranks of Death* (New York, 1947).

3. See, e.g., O. Beall and R. Shryock, *Cotton Mather . . .* (Baltimore, 1954), pp. 46 f.

4. See J. H. Way, "The Clinical History, Nature and Treatment of Milk Sickness," *Amer. Jour. Med. Sciences,* CVI (1893), 307 ff.; G. B. Graff, "The Milk Sickness of the West," *ibid.*, n.s., I (1941), 352. On "cachexia africana," see R. H. Shryock "Medical Practice in the Old South," *South Atlantic Quart.*, XXIX (1930), 160 f.

5. In every year of 1760–1765, inclusive, Christ Church Parish alone reported from 3 to 30 deaths from this disease. Rush remarked of Philadelphia that smallpox was "common, sometimes epidemic," *Medical Inquiries and Observations* (4th ed.; Philadelphia, 1815), Vol. II, p. 231.

6. St. Julien R. Childs, "Health and Disease in the Early History of South Carolina" (M.A. thesis, George Washington Univ., 1931), pp. 24, 40. See also his *Malaria and Colonization in the Carolina Low Country: 1526–1696* (Baltimore, 1940), *passim.*

7. Mrs. Harold Shugg (née Clapesattle) is making a study of the health factor in American population mobility.

8. David Ramsay, *A Review of the Improvements, Progress and State of Medicine in the XVIIIth Century* (Charleston, 1801), pp. 31 f.

9. See, e.g., *Friendly Cautions to the Heads of Families . . .* (Philadelphia, 1804; original ed., 1778), p. 82.

10. Rush, *op. cit.*, pp. 228–235.

11. Beall and Shryock, *op. cit.*, pp. 192–195; W. Blanton, *Medicine in Virginia in the Seventeenth Century* (Richmond, 1930), pp. 47–50.

12. R. O. Cummings, *The American and His Food* (Chicago, 1940), pp. 10–22.

13. C. Bridenbaugh, "Baths and Watering Places in Colonial America," *William and Mary Quart.*, 3rd series, III (1946), 151–181; H. E. Sigerist, "Rise and Fall of the American Spa," *Ciba Symposia,* VIII (1946), 313–326.

14. T. J. Wertenbaker, *First Americans* (New York, 1938), p. 273.

15. Rush, *op. cit.*, pp. 234 f.

16. C. K. Drinker (ed.), *Not So Long Ago* (New York, 1937), p. 29.

17. In the *Herald of Health,* n.s., VI (1865), 109.

18. See, e.g., *Youthful Recreations* (Philadelphia, 1810), *passim.*

19. Norman Himes, *Medical History of Contraception* (Baltimore, 1936), chap. 1.

20. For a human picture of these perils see Drinker, *op. cit.*, chap. 3 on "childbearing in 1790."

21. In the 1760's in Philadelphia from three to six women died in childbed each year in Christ Church Parish alone.

22. Beall and Shryock, *op. cit.*, p. 189.

23. See O. G. Simmons, *Social Status and Public Health,* Soc. Science Research Council, Pamphlet 13 (New York, 1958), pp. 2–7. The verse is quoted in A. M. Stackhouse, *Maladies . . . of Colonial Days in Burlington County* (Moorestown, N.J., 1908), p. 10.

24. Quoted in J. H. Powell, *Bring Out Your Dead* (Philadelphia, 1949), p. 276—the most effective account of any single American epidemic. See also R. H. Shryock, "The Yellow Fever Epidemics, 1793–1905," in Daniel Aaron (ed.), *America in Crisis* (New York, 1952), pp. 51–70; C.-E. A. Winslow, *Conquest of Epidemic Disease* . . . (Princeton, 1943), chap. 11.

25. See R. H. Shryock, "Medical Sources and the Social Historian," *Amer. Hist. Rev.*, XLI (1936), p. 462; J. Duffy, *Epidemics in Colonial America* (Baton Rouge, La., 1953), p. 238.

26. On the parallel European situation, see R. H. Shryock, *The National Tuberculosis Association,* New York, 1957, pp. 30–32.

27. Beall and Shryock, *op. cit.*, p. 85.

28. Unusually careful analyses of New England diphtheria epidemics appear in the papers of Ernest Caulfield; notably in "The Pursuit of a Pestilence," *Amer. Antiq. Soc. Proceeds.*, LX (1950), 121–152. Accounts for given provinces are presented in state medical histories, notably in Vols. I and II of W. Blanton's *Virginia.* J. Duffy's *Epidemics in Colonial America* provides an over-all study.

29. See John Sinclair, *Rules of Health and Longevity* (Edinburgh, 1808), *passim.*

30. George Rosen, "The Fate of the Concept of Medical Police, 1780–1890," *Centaurus,* V (1957), 97–99.

31. M. C. Buer, *Health, Wealth, and Population in the Early Days of the Industrial Revolution* (London, 1926), pp. 143 ff.; Ernest Caulfield, *The Infant Welfare Movement in the Eighteenth Century* (New York, 1931), pp. 140 ff.; G. F. McClearly, *The Early History of the Infant Welfare Movement* (London, 1933), pp. 7–45.

32. J. Brownlee, "The Health of London in the Eighteenth Century," *Roy. Soc. of Med. Proceeds.*, Pt. 2, XVIII (1925), 74.

33. Monica Kiefer, *American Children Through Their Books, 1700–1835* (Philadelphia, 1948), pp. 6 ff.

34. B. Grosvenor, D.D., *Health, An Essay* . . . (3rd ed., Boston, 1761).

35. Ramsay, *op. cit.*, p. 26.

36. Philadelphia bills of mortality, 1807–1817; E. R. Long, "Trends in . . .

Causes of Death in Philadelphia . . . ," *Archives of Pathology*, XXV (1938), 918 ff.

37. Letter to Joseph Priestley, Passy, 1780, in W. T. Franklin (ed.), *Private Correspondence of Benjamin Franklin* (2nd ed.; London, 1817), Vol. I, p. 52.

38. See, e.g., C.-E. A. Winslow, *Health Legislation in Colonial Connecticut* (New Haven, n.d.), pp. 11 ff.

39. W. G. Smillie, *Public Health: Its Promise for the Future* (New York, 1955), p. 77.

40. C. Bridenbaugh, *Cities in the Wilderness* (New York, 1938), p. 159.

41. Bridenbaugh (ed.), "Dr. Thomas Bond's Essay on . . . Clinical Lectures" (1766), *Jour. of the Hist. of Med.*, II (1947).

42. N. M. Blake, *Water for the Cities* (Syracuse, 1956), pp. 15 f. On sanitary arrangements in colonial towns see Bridenbaugh, *Cities in the Wilderness, passim.*

43. See, e.g., Charles Caldwell, *Autobiography* (Philadelphia, 1855), pp. 252–254.

44. Blake, *op. cit.*, chaps, 2, 3, 4.

45. *Medical Inquiries and Observations* (4th ed.; Philadelphia, 1815), Vol. II, p. 237.

46. N. M. Blake, *op. cit.*, pp. 258–260.

47. Albert Deutsch, "The Sick Poor in Colonial Times," *Amer. Hist. Rev.*, XLVI (1941).

48. George Rosen, "An Eighteenth Century Plan for a National Health Service," *Bull. Med. Hist.*, XVI (1944), 429 ff.

49. F. Eden, *State of the Poor* (London, 1797), Vol. I, pp. 603 ff.

50. Rosen, "Hospitals, Medical Care, and Social Policy during the French Revolution," *Bull. Med. Hist.*, XXX (1956), 139.

51. For an over-all picture see R. H. Shryock, "Medicine and Society in the Nineteenth Century," *Jour. of World History* (UNESCO), V, 1959, pp. 122–124.

52. Vital data are taken from the *Historical Statistics of the United States: 1789–1949* (Bureau of the Census, Washington, D.C., 1949), pp. 27, 45, 47; C. and I. Taeuber, *The Changing Population of the United States* (New York, 1958), pp. 269 ff.

53. See, e.g., Peyton Rouse, *The Modern Dance of Death* (Cambridge, 1929), p. 48.

54. Wertenbaker, *op. cit.*, pp. 181 f.

55. Beall and Shryock, *op. cit.*, p. 76.

56. The estimated figures for London are given in John Brownlee, "The Health of London in the Eighteenth Century," *Royal Soc. of Med. Proceeds.*, Pt. 2, XVIII (1925), 76.

57. See J. Duffy (ed.), *The Rudolph Matas History of Medicine in Louisiana* (Baton Rouge, 1958), Vol. I, pp. 269–275.

IV

Medicine and Society in Transition 1820–1860

IN 1765 Dr. John Morgan heralded the appearance in America of true physicians, who would establish here a profession worthy of public esteem. This guild, he believed, would not only improve practice but would advance scientific knowledge to the benefit of all future generations.[1] Yet some seventy-five years later journals were lamenting the "declining state" of the medical profession, and a prominent doctor declared that "not one man" in the United States was doing significant medical research.[2]

In 1789 Dr. Benjamin Rush announced that all previous schemes of physic were faulty but that he was formulating a system which would be more simple, consistent, and effective "than the world had yet seen." Physicians at home and abroad joined in their admiration for this American prodigy.[3] Yet only a half century later, a distinguished thinker—reconsidering Rush's essays—observed that ". . . in the whole vast compass of medical literature, there cannot be found an equal number of pages containing a greater amount and variety of utter nonsense and unqualified absurdity."[4]

In 1801 Dr. David Ramsay of Charleston proclaimed recent advances in hygiene and hailed the prospects for further improving health throughout the United States. Yet less than forty years after these statements were made it became clear that mortality rates in American cities were rising ominously.[5]

Thus in respect to the themes of each of the preceding chapters—the medical profession, medical science, and public health—self-confidence during the Enlightenment was apparently followed by protest and disillusionment in early Victorian days. As will be noted, there were good grounds for these reactions in certain cases. In other connections, however, one must make allowance for the disparagement which a new generation heaps upon the preceding one. Moreover, even when Victorian pessimism was well grounded it was not necessarily inconsistent with medical progress. Protests may have indicated not that matters were worsening but just that men were raising their sights. And disillusionment might clear the way for real achievements.

The optimism of the 1790's had been based in part on actualities which cannot be questioned. A beginning had been made in training an American profession, there had been notable discoveries abroad in medical science, and there probably had been a slight decline in child mortality in this country. Symbolic of medical progress by 1800 was vaccination against smallpox, which was as tangible a contribution to welfare as was, for example, the development of the steam engine in technology.

It is now clear, nevertheless, that medical optimism about 1800 was inflated by the cultural atmosphere of the period. Advances in physical science and in social welfare had promoted faith in progress at large and this faith carried over into medical thinking. By resort to reason, it was held, man was going forward to bigger and better things—in medicine as in other human affairs.

Recall also that American physicians had been further inspired by political upheavals. Medical men had been quite active during the Revolution and had emerged with a fervent belief in the future of their country in general and of its medicine in particular. The connection between the two was well brought out by one of Rush's biographers, who declared:

> The same hand which subscribed the declaration of the political independence of these States, accomplished their emancipation from medical systems formed in foreign countries, and wholly unsuited to the state of diseases in America.

The writings of Rush, of Ramsay, and of others reflected, in their medical patriotism, a state close to professional euphoria. This later made them fair game for more critical successors. Oliver Wendell Holmes, taking Rush apart some fifty years later, remarked that the Philadelphian:

> . . . could not help feeling as if Nature had been a good deal shaken by the Declaration of Independence, and that American art was getting to be rather too much for her,—especially as illustrated in his own practice.[6]

Although revolutionary fervor waned as time passed, it foreshadowed a change in general outlook which was also to have implications for medicine. In most matters eighteenth-century thinkers had evoked reason and had distrusted what they termed "enthusiasm." This calmly rational outlook had been reflected in their devotion to exact science, in their didactic literature, and in their taste for classical balance in the arts.

In search of variety, or perhaps in response to stirring events of the time, attitudes began to change about the turn of the century. Increasingly men yearned for a warmer and less detached state of mind: they envisaged life in terms of adventure rather than of cold analysis. One discerns this most readily in literature and the fine arts, which became suffused with emotion. The didactic Pope gave way to the mystical Coleridge, the impassioned Shelley, and the lovelorn Keats. And the majestic Handel was followed by Wagner, lyric in *Die Meistersinger* and wild in the whirlwind of *Die Valkyrie*. In this age it was no longer enough to be enlightened: men wished to feel deeply, to commit their hearts as well as their minds. In short, romanticism took over.

In recalling exalted expressions of this *Zeitgeist,* one may forget its less lovely popularizations. Devoted patriotism could descend, in this country, to the jingoism of 1812 and of the Mexican War; true sentiment, to the sentimentality of "hearts and flowers"; and genuine grief, to the maudlin banalities of the "tombstone school." Last but not least, for the present purpose, respect for the human body and a sense of delicacy—wherein there were real advances over preceding centuries—were sometimes carried to prudish extremes.

These trends, familiar enough, are recalled here because they had some bearing on medicine. The latter, immersed in early Victorian society, could hardly escape transformations in its environment. But just what were the consequences? In attempting an answer it will be best to distinguish between popular responses and those of the medical profession.

Most obvious, among popular reactions, was a tendency to sentimentalize illness—at least those types of illness which lent themselves to the process. Violent and repulsive entities like smallpox or cholera were not amenable, but any disease which permitted onlookers to linger over the victim without shock or injury was appropriate for the purpose.

The chief killer of the time, pulmonary tuberculosis, was made to order in this connection. Its lesions were hidden and the superficial pallor and weakness were thought rather fascinating. The mind remained bright and hopeful; indeed, the disease was said to contribute to genius in promising young men. And a genteel female "going into a decline" symbolized the Victorian ideal of feminine frailty.

Even a doctor, contemplating his favorite case of consumption, would forget "the churchyard cough" and note rather the "nearly etherical delicacy" of the victim—as well as the "languor in the azure eyes . . . which told of something too refined for humanity." [7] Contemporary novels, plays, and operas were so given to sweet-sad musings of this sort that consumption may be said to have made a morbid contribution to art and letters.

There is no evidence that sentimentality of this sort did much harm. Quite otherwise was the effect of another kind of exaggerated sensitivity, that of the prudery just mentioned. Middle- and upper-class women often declined to consult physicians for gynecologic services, except as a last resort. Note the implications of the following letter, written by the first secretary of the A.M.A. from Savannah, in 1838, to Dr. Charles Meigs of Philadelphia:

> . . . I cannot give any further information beyond what you could yourself obtain from Mrs. ——. As the wife of a medical man, she is aware that false delicacy too often injures females, by their allowing disease to get beyond the reach of medical art before they speak out. I have told her to answer any question you should think necessary to ask her.[8]

The Dr. Meigs mentioned above, by the way, carried Victorian sentimentality over into his writings. He referred to patients as "the dear little ladies"—an expression one would hardly encounter today. But his opinion of these ladies indicates why women had such an uphill struggle to re-enter the medical profession. Woman, Dr. Meigs informed his students, has no part in affairs of the mind. Home, rather, is her place, "except when, like the Star of day, she deigns to issue forth—to exhibit her beauty and her grace." She has, he concluded, "a head almost too small for intellect but just big enough for love." All this, believe it or not, appeared in a textbook on obstetrics.[9]

The reference to the size of women's heads makes more sense if one recalls the then-current vogue of phrenology. Originating in the anatomic studies of Gall, which are usually viewed as the first investigations of cerebral localization, phrenology became a popular cult which was supported by many leading figures—including some medical men. It had no direct bearing on the healing art, though its popularity has been viewed as analogous to the later vogue of psychoanalysis.[10] But phrenology did illustrate the lure which grandiose, pseudo-scientific doctrines held for this age. All problems could be solved by some adventurous, new solution which promised the millennium.

Health, inevitably, was central to some of these programs. Mesmerism touched upon it. After being rejected in scientific circles in the 1780's, it continued to attract popular attention during the next century and apparently played a part later in the origins of Christian Science. More sweeping were the health cults which promised all things if men would only observe certain "rules of life" and stay away from the doctors. Such were the teachings, for example, of Sylvester Graham, whose name survives today in Graham crackers.[11] Cultists of this type breathed a romantic fervor into personal hygiene, hitherto a medical theme. They made a secular religion of health, and their disciples—subsisting on vegetables and bran--led a truly austere life in its name.

Sentimentalists invaded still other areas hitherto reserved largely for medical men. Notable was the temperance movement, initiated by physicians during the 1700's as a more or less scientific campaign against alcoholism.[12] From about the 1820's on, leadership was taken over by the clergy and other moral reformers, who transformed a problem into a "cause" and so infused into it an emotionalism quite alien to the original movement.

It is difficult to discern any patterns in doctor-patient relationships which reflected a sentimental outlook. Some families had great confidence in their practitioners, others abandoned them in favor of rivals or sectarians. If one may judge by the rareness of gifts to physicians or to medical schools, however, there was no inclination to look upon medical men as the saviors of mankind.[13]

The truth is that the romantic spirit had little to work upon here. There was no such confidence in medical personnel as is suggested by modern allusions to "men in white" or "women in white," and medical schools were viewed as self-supporting concerns. When given a chance, however, sentiment did invade medical institutions, as may be observed in the vision of the "lady with a lamp" evoked by Florence Nightingale in 1859. Similar feeling was associated with Dorothea Dix and other "angels of mercy" who performed nursing services during the Civil War.

One may sum up at this point by saying that romanticism influenced popular attitudes toward disease, permeated health crusades without benefit of doctors, and lent its light to certain medical services. But none of these phenomena answer the question originally posed; that is, why all the disillusionment after 1820 concerning medical research, the medical profession, and public health in the United States? Let us then consider actual developments in each of these areas between about 1820 and 1860.

In regard to medical science one can readily understand disillusionment concerning claims for a peculiarly American medicine. Faith in this dogma waned with the loss of revolutionary zeal. Curiously enough, the whole argument was revived after 1840 within more narrow geographic limits. As political tensions grew between North and South, southern doctors began talking about diseases peculiar to their section and the consequent need for a truly southern medicine. Just as their grandfathers had urged independence from British medical schools, so *they* demanded a break with Yankee colleges. The resulting controversy, however, was tangential to the real history of medical science and was largely forgotten after 1865.

A second type of disillusionment, that concerning rival "systems" of medical theory and practice, requires more careful explanations. It will be recalled that Rush, for example, claimed to have improved upon the views of Cullen and of Brown; and other Americans then elaborated on *his* theories or even announced more perfect syntheses.[14] In each case all diseases were said to inhere in some common, underlying reaction; and one, basic type of treatment was deduced from the premises. One would have expected such theories to flourish in the romantic atmosphere of the 1830's and forties. They were grandiose and adventurous: there was nothing piecemeal or prosaic about them. And flourish they did—in a somewhat unexpected manner.

In order to understand subsequent trends, however, attention again must be shifted from America to the European background.

There, in large measure, the future of medical science unfolded. Extraordinary changes were under way between 1800 and 1840, notably in the so-called "Paris school."

Continued attempts were made abroad to identify specific diseases in terms of a localized, structural pathology; in other words, by correlating bedside symptoms with lesions observed at autopsies. Morgagni had given a lead here, and even such a theorist as Cullen had recognized the significance of pathologic anatomy. But other influences converged on Paris in the early 1800's, notably the growing vogue of empirical philosophy, the example of the physical sciences, and even the structural implications of surgery. Reorganization of faculties, hospitals, and other institutions under Napoleon also had its advantages in implementing large-scale investigations.[15]

In consequence of these circumstances something like systematic medical research appeared for the first time. The same hospital physician acted as both clinician and pathologist and sought to correlate ante-mortem symptoms with post-mortem findings. The process necessitated more careful bedside studies: patients were thereafter examined rather than merely observed. Hence instruments to aid examination were developed—such as the stethoscope, which has remained ever since a symbol of the profession. And autopsies, instead of being occasional as heretofore, became routine. Only in these ways could certain diseases be so studied as to make clear identifications possible.

In all this, clinicians became as "objective" as the human nature of their materials permitted. Focusing on specific diseases in themselves, they lost interest in the body's generalized responses and even in the patient as a person. They dealt no longer with the pathetic Mr. —— in Ward B but rather with the classic case of tuberculosis in that same repository.

This was a relatively cold-blooded approach to human illness but it brought results. What had been vaguely termed "inflammation of the chest," for example, was broken down—by distinct lesions and related symptoms—into the more specific concepts of pneumonia, pleurisy, bronchitis, and so on. Such discoveries, it must be admitted, were of little aid to the sick. French clinicians were not seeking remedies in the traditional manner; instead, they became skeptical about even such treatments as had long been taken for granted. Hence, from the patients' viewpoint, they took away the old therapy before there was much to put in its place.

The Parisians worked almost as pure scientists without much immediate concern about useful results. Their data were provided by generations of poor folk in the wards, whose unwitting contributions are now largely forgotten. Whether the fact that most autopsies were performed on subjects from this same class affected the resulting pictures of disease is difficult to say. In any case, pure science "paid off" in the long run. Obviously, rational means for preventing or curing specific diseases could never have been found until the diseases themselves had first been identified.

Not so obvious but equally true was the fact that disease identifications were necessary to any critical examination of modes of treatment. The idea that therapy might be checked by statistics, even as were public health conditions, had occurred to a few observers during the preceding century. The layman William Cobbett, for example, had sought to refute Rush's practice by resort to the bills of mortality in 1793. But actual clinical statistics were meaningless until one was reasonably sure about diagnoses. It was not until the 1820's, after French clinicians had secured clearer concepts of entities, that Pierre Louis advocated the use of a "numerical method" in checking on bleeding and purging. Although his method had technical limitations, its introduction was another major step in bringing the potent influence of quantification into medical science.[16]

The Parisian program was apparently a triumph for medical empiricism—long preached but rarely practiced except in sporadic fashion. But the very fact that there *was* a program, as we now see it, marked French research off from what had often been called empiricism in the past. Frequently insistence on "facts" and aversion to theories had been associated with little more than a trial-and-error quest for remedies. When an American disciple exclaimed in 1824 that the search for remedies had "led nowhere," he was repudiating this more naïve type of empiricism.

Such a reaction was doubtless too extreme; the most valuable drugs then known had been discovered by trial-and-error methods. But progress by these means had been extremely slow and haphazard, whereas French leaders maintained the faith that rational science would speed up and extend the whole process. Moreover, despite an aversion to theories and a demand for verification, their whole outlook was based on the assumption that diseases were objective realities. This "ontologic" concept, discussed in a preceding chapter, was axiomatic rather than verifiable and came close to being metaphysical in nature. In a word, French clinicians were empiricists but by no means "mere empirics."

As might be expected, the Paris school was not responsive to romantic enthusiasms. German medical thinkers, influenced by Kantian idealism, were given between 1810 and 1830 to a speculative *Naturphilosophie* which is usually called "romantic medicine"; and a similar transcendentalism reached into English and American literature. French and British clinicians, in contrast, remained cold-blooded realists. Naturalists and astronomers might enthuse with Kant over "the starry heavens above" but pathologists did not find *their* observations quite so inspiring.

It may be added that American clinicians, in major city hospitals, maintained much the same attitude as did their French and British colleagues. It is true that some doctors in the States were influenced by romantic idealism, and such men hid their lack of originality behind a metaphysical façade—as in orating solemnly on "Nature and Nature's God." But when works expressing such an outlook were reviewed their contents were likely to be dismissed as "almost transcendental abstractions."

The fame of Parisian leaders was spread first by their own publications, then by foreign journals. In Philadelphia, for example, the *Eclectic Repertory*—founded in 1810—changed its name to the

Journal of Foreign Medical Science. From 1810 to 1815 its issues were still devoted to reprints from British periodicals; between 1815 and 1820 a few French items appeared; and then, in 1821, there was a deluge of Parisian material. Nothing like this research program had been heard of before and it seems to have carried conviction almost from the start. Claims about the superiority of American medicine were rarely heard after the latter year. The Philadelphia faculty soon expressed doubts about Rush's "conjectures" and condemned David Hosack of New York for reviving the "obsolete creed" of humoralism.[17] There were similar reactions in New York and New England medical centers. In New Haven, for example, Nathan Smith rejected Rush's whole outlook in the course of writing his able paper on "typhus fever" (typhoid) in 1824.

No doubt there was some opposition at first from "old school" physicians. Rush's views were still praised on one or two occasions before medical societies during the twenties, but such speakers were already on the defensive.[18] In 1820 a paper appeared in Philadelphia which condemned hospital studies in principle as "a particularly dangerous form" of empiricism, but this seems to have been one of the last rear-guard actions on the part of regular physicians.[19]

Inspired by French reports, a few American students departed for Paris in the 1820's and more followed them in the thirties. That city soon replaced London as the medical Mecca, chiefly on its merits but partly because of lingering, Revolutionary feeling. It was easier to accept French leadership than to return to dependence on the mother country. Meantime British attitudes toward American physicians underwent a subtle change—now that the latter were foreigners rather than colonials who needed encouragement. The sympathetic interest of a Fothergill was replaced by Sydney Smith's strident question: "What does the world yet owe to American physicians and surgeons?" (1820).[20] It is true that the common language made for a continued use of British texts in the United States, but there was nevertheless a conscious shift of professional interest from London to Paris.

The next step was to attempt pathologic research in the Gallic manner. The basic idea was not new: Dr. Bond had advocated it in the 1760's, and Americans must have known Matthew Baillie's pioneer English text on morbid anatomy of 1793. But it was the French example that inspired a few Americans really to do something in this field.

In 1820, during a yellow fever epidemic in Philadelphia, autopsies were performed on most of the victims, whereas, in preceding outbreaks, the procedure had been an occasional one. Shortly thereafter "the Philadelphia Anatomy Rooms" were opened and dissections there became more frequent. Dr. John D. Godman, who directed them, gave considerable attention to morbid anatomy and he was apparently the first American to publish on the subject. His modest writings of 1824 and '25 were not outstanding but indicated an attempt to do original work. More ambitious was a book on pathology published in 1829 by William Horner—usually said to have been the first American work in its field.

Dr. Godman had been editor of the *Journal of Foreign Medical Science,* and it was probably no accident that one of the first Americans to search the Parisian literature was also the first to practice what was therein preached. He was quite aware of the implications. Medicine, declared Godman in 1824, was at least two centuries behind the point it could have reached had it only persevered in the pathologic research inaugurated during the Renaissance. Instead, physicians had searched for remedies and this "led nowhere." Now medical science had to begin all over again in the work of the Paris school, which was worth more than all other medical research from Hippocrates to Rush! [21]

Dr. Samuel Jackson, associated with Godman, supported the latter's view and analyzed the situation briefly in his *Principles of Medicine* (1832). He agreed that speculative approaches were outmoded. Familiar with the writings of the philosopher Comte, Jackson held that system-makers operated on the "metaphysical" level but that pathologic research would soon raise medical science to the "positive" plane.[22] The most thorough presentation of the French outlook came with the next decade, however, when Elisha Bartlett—

a New Englander—published his *Philosophy of Medical Science* (1844). By that time the reaction against theories was such that Bartlett condemned all hypotheses and even distrusted inductive reasoning. He desired only "facts," which were apparently to speak for themselves. In a word, he carried French empiricism to its logical extreme.[23]

By the early 1830's American physicians were returning to the States after postgraduate training in Paris. Those who found themselves in isolated practice, like Osler's "Alabama Student," were unable to accomplish much, but a number who established themselves in the chief cities made creditable studies in pathologic anatomy. James Jackson the younger, a former pupil of Pierre Louis, might have introduced in Boston his mentor's hope for full-time research—had it not been for his untimely death. But William Gerhardt of Philadelphia distinguished clearly between typhoid and typhus on the basis of clinical-anatomic correlations (1837); and similar research was done by Alfred Stillé in that city and by James Jackson and George B. Shattuck in Boston. Two years later Samuel Gross published a work hailed by one European scholar as the first adequate pathology text in any language.[24]

French medicine, of course, involved more than a focus on clinical-pathologic studies and an emphasis on empiricism. Magendie, carrying on in the tradition of Haller, threw light on the physiology of nerves by systematic animal experimentation. But "anatomic thinking" dominated physiology as well as pathology in this era; that is, it was assumed that functions could be best discovered by inference from structures rather than by experiment on living subjects. Hence there were few physiologic studies of a modern type before the 1840's. The research of William Beaumont in this country stands out not only because of its brilliance but also because it was rare. Taking advantage of an accident which produced a permanent fistula in a patient's stomach, Beaumont used his perambulating laboratory to demonstrate the chemical nature of gastric digestion in man (1825–1833). His publications attracted favorable attention in Europe but led at the time to no further studies of importance in America.[25]

French medicine also contributed specific methods of research which grew out of its clinical orientation, for example, the use of instruments of observation and the employment of clinical statistics. Stethoscopes were known in American cities in the 1820's, though Godman complained in '24 that they were not yet used extensively. Strangely enough, there was a long delay in introducing the pulse watch and the clinical thermometer—in Europe as well as in America. Karl Wunderlich of Leipzig finally established the use of the latter in the 1850's, but it was still a rare instrument in this country during the Civil War era.[26] Meantime, Louis's "numerical method" seems to have been accepted in the United States, in principle, as early as 1828. And one finds attempts to use clinical statistics in the American literature of the 1840's.[27]

French activities in the field of mental health, after the publication of Pinel's basic study (1801) and during the subsequent work of his pupil E. D. Esquirol, were known to American physicians interested in psychiatry. The statement sometimes made that no general work on the subject was published here between 1812 and late in the century is not true, since Thomas C. Upham of Bowdoin College brought out a comprehensive study in 1840. But Upham was not a physician and he viewed mental illness in the older, philosophic manner rather than in the current, European terms of pathologic anatomy. He was aware of the latter outlook and repudiated it in principle. Now that psychological approaches to this field have been revived, his book is again of some interest.

A few medical men, meanwhile, began to seek for lesions associated with types of mental illness—but with no success. The chief trend in American psychiatry, between 1820 and 1860, related to humane, institutional care rather than to research. The background to this movement was the general humanitarianism of the age, as applied by such Europeans as Tuke and Pinel and by the American Rush to the treatment of mental patients. In due time many "asylums" were provided for "the insane" and these will be noted in commenting on the hospitals of the time.

Of immediate concern to American practitioners were limited

advances in pharmacology. The analytic chemistry of the period contributed several new drugs derived from plant products which proved of considerable value; for example, morphine was isolated from opium in 1804 and introduced into general practice in the forties—along with the first hypodermic needles. And during the 1820's, meantime, French chemists had isolated strychnine from nux vomica and quinine from cinchona bark. Quinine was particularly useful in the United States, where by the 1840's large doses were providing a more effective control of malaria than had hitherto been available.

Despite these achievements, as noted, French clinicians became skeptical about most old drugs and procedures, and this attitude was carried to the extremes of "clinical nihilism" in some countries influenced by the French example.

There had always been physicians who left much to nature in the treatment of illness. Nathan Smith, for example, had advocated such a procedure in the 1820's. But the first effective protest against heroic practice in the United States seems to have been that voiced in Jacob Bigelow's paper "On Self-Limited Diseases"—read at Boston in 1835. Bigelow was a former student of Rush, but his native New England never seems to have been so dominated by the latter's methods as were the states to the south and west.

There was evidence by that time, in some parts of the country, that Rush's treatments were being carried to even greater extremes. Thus, John E. Cooke of Lexington, Kentucky, wrote that Rush had been "vilified" for giving ten grains of the purgative jalap, while "now (1833) thousands of physicians administer up to 100 grains." Cooke encouraged such dosing, not only for cures but even for prophylaxis. Pioneer farmers were pictured as living on bread and calomel in the place of bread and butter.[28]

One can readily understand Dr. Bigelow's protest in the face of these circumstances. Other medical leaders soon expressed similar views. As an example of such "nihilism" consider Dr. Samuel Jackson's statement of 1840: "The least important part of the science . . . is the dosing of patients with medicine." Patients might be "amused" by imaginary remedies, he thought, while nature provided the real cures.[29] In a word, heroic practice elicited equally extreme denials of the value of medication.

As if to offset the loss of faith in internal medicine, marked progress was made in surgery during the first half of the nineteenth century. Here, again, the focus on pathologic anatomy was essential. As long as humoral or tension theories held sway, surgeons had no grounds for interfering in most disease processes; but the localized, structural pathology of the 1830's and forties held out more promise for surgical intervention. Between 1810 and 1840 G. Dupuytren and other French surgeons removed such organs as the thyroid gland and the uterus; and, in England, Sir Benjamin Brodie's works on the diseases of joints (1818) and on urology (1832) extended the province of surgery beyond the limits of the preceding century.[30]

The skill and daring displayed by some American surgeons, during the first half of the nineteenth century, has often been ascribed to isolation. Practitioners so situated, it is held, were not bound by tradition and developed confidence in their own resources. Dr. Ephraim McDowell's pioneer ovariotomy, performed in Kentucky in 1809, is often cited as an illustration of this thesis. But McDowell, like most other Americans distinguished for their surgery in the period before 1840, had been trained abroad. Much of the best surgery of the day, moreover, was performed in New York and Philadelphia—a fact which hardly fits into the frontier hypothesis.

Dr. Physick in Philadelphia, for example, was famed for his lithotomies, his instrument used in tonsillectomies, and his introduction of buckskin sutures. In New York, subsequently, Valentine Mott became noted for his repair of difficult aneurysms. Samuel Gross later declared that Americans were outstanding in such surgery of the blood vessels, as well as in that relating to the long bones and joints. Probably the most useful achievement in American surgery, however, was the successful operation for vaginal fistula introduced by J. Marion Sims of Mobile in 1849; and American gynecology was thereafter outstanding.[31]

It will be observed that surgery rarely invaded the chief body cavities. The difficulties of operating on conscious patients and the near-certainty of fatal infection precluded such major operations. Surgery, both in homes and in hospitals, continued to be a grim business until the introduction of anesthesia.[32] This latter event was the outcome of a number of circumstances—the increasing interest in surgery at large, the growth of humanitarian concern, the discovery of new chemicals, and the particular needs of dental surgery.

As is well known it was a dentist, W. T. G. Morton, rather than a surgeon, who introduced ether anesthesia at the Massachusetts General in 1846. One might explain the fact, somewhat cynically, by noting that dentists urged patients to return for further treatments and so were particularly interested in overcoming fear of pain. In contrast, surgeons—under prevailing circumstances—rarely expected to treat a patient more than once.

Be that as it may, inhalation anesthesia was rapidly adopted throughout the Western world. It was a great technical achievement in improving the conditions faced by surgeons and at the same time was a milestone in the history of humanitarianism. One may well view anesthesia as the chief contribution of American medical men during the nineteenth century.[33]

Parenthetically, the role of dentists in the story of anesthesia recalls the rapid development of dental surgery in the United States after about 1830. The original impetus for this had come from French army surgeons present in America during and after the Revolution, but Americans seem to have taken a special interest in this nascent specialty. By the 1830's Dr. Horace Hayden was lecturing on dental surgery in the medical school of the University of Maryland and in 1840 helped to establish the pioneer Baltimore College of Dental Surgery. No such concern with dentistry had yet appeared abroad; and thereafter American dentists tended to surpass the European, both in the making of false teeth and in the preserving of natural ones. The Americans even invaded Europe after 1840, thus reversing for the first time the usual direction of cultural exchange between the two continents.[34]

The other great obstacle to major surgery, infection, was not even partially overcome until the 1860's in the work of the British surgeon Lister. Demands for cleanliness in the related field of obstetrics were made in the 1840's, by both Semmelweis in Vienna and Oliver Wendell Holmes in Boston. But these efforts accomplished little, partly because physicians resented the charge that they themselves conveyed puerperal fever and partly because there was as yet no general understanding of the nature of infection.

The problem of infection received increasing attention, however, by the 1840's. Despite a prevailing belief in miasmata as causes of epidemics, the old animalcular theory was revived by the use of improved microscopes in the study of minute organisms. In Europe, this interest originated in laboratory observations (as in Ehrenberg's work on infusoria, 1830) and then led to controlled studies of "germs" involved in particular diseases. In the United States, however, the idea was picked up by those concerned with epidemiology.

Interest in the environmental aspects of disease had been keen in this country since the 1790's, and a half century later many articles appeared "on the fevers" of a particular county or region. The great achievement in this area was the publication of Daniel Drake's *Diseases of the Interior Valley of North America* (1850)—a monumental contribution to what is now sometimes called geomedicine.

In the course of studying the spread and distribution of diseases over a given area, Drake, J. K. Mitchell, Josiah Nott, and other Americans decided that a *contagium vivum* could best explain the phenomena observed.[35] The data, as far as they went, were sound, and their reasoning—however much Elisha Bartlett might have disapproved it—was plausible. But since they did not pursue the problem into the laboratory, their thesis could not be confirmed at the time. Subsequently, therefore, interest in the "germ theory" declined in the United States, and when the idea was again brought in from Europe in the 1870's it seemed a new revelation.

The failure of English-speaking countries to set up experimental laboratories, such as Germans were developing by 1850, was an obvious weakness. Observational sciences, such as anatomy, astronomy, and geology, could flourish in the absence of "labs" but not so physiology, chemistry, or nascent bacteriology.[36]

The limitations of medical research in the United States, however, cannot be ascribed entirely to the lack of technical facilities. Despite the acceptance of French concepts in medical centers and despite excellent work on the part of such men as have been mentioned, the general research record by mid-century was not impressive. Important contributions were made to surgery and bedside observations revealed some useful, diagnostic signs. In two or three instances, American medical men produced brilliant but rather isolated results—as in the case of Beaumont. But combined clinical-pathologic studies—then the medical field par excellence—were sporadic and largely peripheral to European advances. Few Americans of this era can be said to have had research careers in medicine; an able man, if he made a discovery, often had the rest of his life swallowed up in practice. And no American cities were research centers in the sense that Paris, London, and Vienna were.

Although there had been some lip service to research since the days of John Morgan, no serious efforts were made to encourage it. Admittedly, the circumstances were difficult, since—the world over—original studies were left to doctors already overburdened with practice. Comte remarked that the situation was analogous to what would have obtained in astronomy if original work in that science had been left to the sea captains. But within these limits there were certain difficulties peculiar to the United States.

For one thing, it is not clear that most medical men—even in the best schools—were fully alerted to the significance of investigations. Professors, in introductory or commencement addresses, orated at length on the duties and ideals of the profession. But, with rare exceptions, it never occurred to them to mention research. And when it *was* mentioned in any connection there were those even in the schools who rather deprecated the idea. As late as 1860 Oliver Wendell Holmes—for all his Paris training—reverted to the ridicule of science as having no value for actual practice.

The few physicians who did envisage research protested vehemently against its neglect. Godman, in the twenties, had ascribed this to the backwardness of medical science in general. But Samuel Jackson, in 1832, sensed that the native situation was partly responsible and blamed the "paucity" and "miserable mismanagement" of hospitals for the lag in pathologic studies.

Jackson returned to this theme a decade later, but by then his explanations had broadened. He began by noting the advent of systematic research in Germany and declared that "not one man" in the United States was engaged in such studies. He now indicted American society as a whole. The essential trouble, he held, was "the commercialism of the age," which led to a worship of wealth and accorded little recognition to intellectual achievements. Physicians, caught up in this environment, depended for prestige as well as for income on successful practice. Even wealthy men, therefore, would not take time off for original work. As a remedy, the Philadelphian beseeched his students to attempt research in their first lean years, ere the shades of money-making closed about them.[37]

These were sweeping conclusions difficult to confirm but they were shared by many nonmedical critics. Emerson and other literary lights had somewhat similar things to say about American society. And it will be recalled that de Tocqueville, who had published his *Democracy in America* in 1835, had emphasized the neglect of "theoretical science"—ascribing this to equalitarian practicality within an expanding economy and to the ease of borrowing from Europe. Although middle-class "commercialism" was sometimes defended in the States,[38] de Tocqueville held that it encouraged only applied science. In aristocratic societies, he declared, science is cultivated to gratify the mind, but in democracies to satisfy the body.[39]

Despite its bluntness, this thesis is plausible when applied to the American record in medical science. It will be noted that physicians in this country excelled in applied research of immediate utility, as in surgery, but were not outstanding in such basic fields as physiology and pathology. Insofar as de Tocqueville's comments were sound, Americans were in a particularly unhappy position with regard to these two latter disciplines. Although we can now see that at this point the future of medical science depended largely on the development of pathology, research in that area was of little use in medical practice as late as the 1850's. It is small wonder that a "practical," relatively democratic society did not encourage it.[40]

Within the general social setting, of course, certain professional developments in the United States also had a bearing on the cultivation of medical research. Before considering these, however, it were well to warn against exaggerating the limitations ascribed above to medical science in this country. Despite the relative lack of originality in certain basic fields, it would be a mistake to ignore what was accomplished in other areas.

Moreover, by the 1840's the general tone of native medical thought had become far more critical than it had been a generation earlier. One has only to compare the journals of the two periods to sense the contrast. The very criticisms voiced by such men as Jackson were a sign of progress, in that they replaced the complacency of post-Revolution decades. American medical leaders at least knew where they stood by 1850 and had some inkling of what must be done if they were to advance in the future. The day was not far distant, it may be added, when basic research would promise utility and Americans would then be prepared—in part by their very "commercialism"—to respond and even to "take over." [41]

More intensive research might conceivably have been carried on in the United States, 1820–1860, if the standards of medical schools and the status of the medical profession had been higher than was actually the case. One would not expect mediocre schools ministering to mediocre personnel to produce much that was original. But there was a vicious circle here, in that advancing research was—as later events showed—the chief factor calculated to improve education and professional standing. Poor schools implied limited research, but only research could raise the standards of the schools. The circle was eventually broken after 1870 by outer rather than inner pressures; that is, by the impact of the latest European science.

It would be a mistake, however, to assume that preceding American developments played no part in the final outcome. The effort to raise the standards of the medical profession, begun in the 1760's, encountered extraordinary difficulties after 1820 but was by no means abandoned thereafter. It was no accident that there were always leaders in the American profession who envisaged a promised land, and who sought a way through the wilderness of mid-century decades toward this ultimate destination. German medical standards did not migrate to America after 1870 because of German efforts or even of their own accord; they were imported, rather, by American leaders who had learned by experience what was needed in their own society and could recognize excellence when they saw it.

Moreover, although the difficulties involved in developing an American profession were extreme, they were similar in kind to those met with abroad. Encountered in European societies as well as in the United States, for example, were the problems posed by sectarianism, by quackery, and by second-class practitioners at large. American experience therefore not only provides background for later events in this country but also helps to document the larger professional history of the nineteenth century.

The chief trends in American medical education after 1820 are well known and need not be recalled here in detail. The first medical schools had been intended to supplement rather than to replace training by apprenticeship and this view still obtained as late as the 1840's. A large proportion of those who entered practice up to about 1820, moreover, did so without benefit of any formal education. One has only to note the small number of schools then available in order to realize that this must have been the case.

At the beginning of the century four medical schools existed—all located in northeastern states. By the twenties medical colleges had also been established in Maryland, Virginia, South Carolina, Kentucky, and Ohio, and additional ones had appeared in the northeastern area. But the total number in the mid-twenties was only about seventeen. All told, these colleges enrolled some 2,000 students each year. This in itself would not have been excessive for a nation whose population was approaching 12 million had it not been for those who entered practice by other routes.[42]

One can understand that, up to this time, the growing number of schools was viewed as a sign of progress. This was all the more true because most of these schools were associated with arts colleges and were devoted to an educational program for its own sake.

As early as 1812, however, the faculty of the Baltimore school became themselves the body corporate of what Norwood calls "the so-called Medical Department of the so-called University of Maryland." This step was interesting for two reasons:

In the first place, it placed the faculty in control of "their own school" and so could be viewed as a return to the "faculty rule" which had originally been envisaged for the first American arts colleges. Unfortunately, however, nothing could have been more dangerous in medical education than faculty ownership, since it opened the door in this particular field to proprietary exploitation.

In the second place, the Baltimore school lacked arts college connections, whatever may have been the hospital facilities to which it had access. Its incorporation therefore may be viewed as a break with the university-college tradition, which Morgan had introduced originally from Scotland and which had been followed elsewhere in the States up to that time. The Baltimore institution looked something like a London hospital school without the thorough integration with a hospital which characterized the latter type of institution.[43]

During the late 1820's and the thirties, the increase in the number of medical colleges accelerated. By 1839 there were thirty or more such colleges in existence and others were being founded each year. A dozen of the best-known schools registered all told nearly 2,000 students, so that one may estimate that the total annual number reached at least 3,000. Pennsylvania had much the greatest enrollment of any one school (444) and was followed by two western (or southern?) colleges—Transylvania at Lexington (257) and a school at Louisville (204). "P. and S." in New York City listed 102 students.

New England schools in contrast remained small, Harvard registering 74 and Yale only 45. In that same year Pennsylvania granted degrees to 163 men, Transylvania to 60, South Carolina to 63, Harvard to 22, and Yale to 15.

The concentration of medical education in the original center, Philadelphia, was evident from the fact that there were now three strong schools there—the University of Pennsylvania, Jefferson Medical College (1825), and the Pennsylvania Medical College (1839)—whose total graduates reached 248.[44] New York City, which had possessed several medical schools between 1810 and 1840, was by 1841 the site of two strong colleges—P. and S. (Columbia) and the newly established school at New York University.

Faculties were growing along with student bodies. Whereas the first medical college had originally had only two chairs, and Nathan Smith had taught all subjects at Dartmouth about 1800, most schools now possessed some five to eight posts in such fields as theory and practice ("medicine"), materia medica, anatomy, surgery, obstetrics, and chemistry. Chairs in physiology and in pathology also began to be established.

It was becoming apparent by this time that the qualitative situation in medical education was a more serious problem than the quantitative. Groups of doctors began to follow the Baltimore precedent in forming their own schools, most of which were operated for profit. An instance of this sort had occurred in Vermont as early as 1818 and others followed. Such proprietary colleges multiplied in the 1840's and the threat to standards was obvious.

The proliferation of schools may have been stimulated by efforts to secure legislation requiring an M.D. of future practitioners. Here one had a continuation of the move toward professional monopoly which was discussed in a preceding chapter. In 1821, for example, a Georgia law restricted practice to men holding a degree.[45] Legislation of this sort, when enforced at all, was less likely to raise standards than it was to encourage the founding of easy schools. But it may have hastened the day when nearly all candidates attended some sort of medical college. The number of men who depended entirely on apprenticeship declined after 1820, though just when it became less than the number who took degrees can hardly be determined.

The lure of low-grade schools was also increased by the tendency to follow Massachusetts in granting licensing power to faculties. New York, for example, authorized medical schools to license graduates in 1814, and by 1826 a president of the State Medical Society warned of the dangers involved. Already, he held, some degrees required less of the student than did the examination given to apprentice-trained candidates.[46] In a word, an easy school provided a highroad to the right to practice.

Legislatures were inclined to grant charters to any groups of physicians who desired them. Was not the United States by this time a free society, in which competition was the life of trade and also of professions which—if not actually trades—were something close to them? Since professors continued to practice and receive student fees in addition, a school added to their income and meantime needed little support from the community. Few facilities were needed other than a modest building, and the faculty themselves often provided that. Everyone was happy about such arrangements except those who worried about standards.

The first sign that standards were falling had appeared as early as 1789, when the College of Philadelphia had given up the premedical requirements originally introduced by Morgan. The move apparently resulted from competition with the then rival school of the University of the State of Pennsylvania; and thereafter, in large cities, such competition between two or more local institutions continued to inhibit strict requirements.

Equally serious was the fact that outside of Philadelphia—and later in New York and Boston—clinical facilities were inadequate or even nonexistent. Hospital connections, when available at all, were casual, and many schools depended on their own small infirmaries. The teaching of anatomy was, in many places, limited to demonstrations—since the securing of subjects was still difficult if not dangerous. In general, emphasis was placed on didactic lectures. Although a course of two years was required in the better schools, the second was just a repetition of the first.

In view of the lack of clinical teaching, there was some merit in the founding—late in the period under consideration—of the first genuine hospital schools in this country. Several medical colleges grew into hospital schools when they finally built their own hospitals, as did Jefferson in 1847. But the first colleges to be established *within* hospitals in the London manner were those set up about 1860 by the Long Island College Hospital in Brooklyn and by the Bellevue Hospital Medical College in New York City. Such schools could, by their very nature, provide ample clinical facilities, and within a decade Bellevue became one of the strongest institutions in the country.[47]

Looking back more than half a century later, Dr. William H. Welch thought that imitation of the London hospital schools had proved a major weakness in American medical education. He had in mind the stimulating and restraining influences which could be provided by university affiliation—the values which Morgan had originally had in mind. But it must be remembered that the connections which early medical schools had with arts colleges were nominal at best. Medical faculties were quite independent, and the associated arts faculties had practically no influence upon them. Only Yale seems to have been an exception to this rule; there the small medical enrollments have been ascribed to the standards maintained by Yale College. Later, of course, university affiliation became a more meaningful matter, and it will be noted that the Bellevue school was eventually merged with New York University.

When proprietary schools multiplied after 1840, the efforts of the older colleges to maintain training standards became even more difficult. Seeking large enrollments and consequent profits, some of the proprietary faculties sought to make medical training as quick and easy as possible. Such competition was difficult to meet: when Pennsylvania sought at one time to tighten requirements, students were reported to be leaving for "easier quarters."

How difficult the situation became is suggested by the correspondence of Dr. Richard Arnold, one of the two first secretaries of the A.M.A. and a professor in a reputable college in Savannah. In 1857 he wrote a friend in New York:

> We have taken the first bold, unequivocal stand against a growing abuse, viz. taking a winter student, hurrying him through a summer course, & turning him out a doctor in less than a year. . . . This has been done by Oglethorpe College here. . . . The Atlanta College avows and defends this course. Sir, you are one of our Pilots . . . You won golden opinions at Nashville by your defense of our Profession as it was formerly educated. Has not that day passed away? When schools can act in this way & Professors . . . talk as some talked, are we not fallen upon evil days? As God is my judge I speak for the Profession at large & not for our College.[48]

Superimposed upon all these difficulties within the medical profession were those associated with the rise of sectarianism and with the proliferation of quackery. The latter reached its heyday in the mid-nineteenth century, both in the United States and abroad. The small-scale patent medicine business of the later 1700's swelled into wholesale concerns which made millions by introducing national advertising in newspapers and magazines. They found secret, tradename panaceas preferable to time-limited patents and saturated even family and religious magazines with "ads" of their infallible remedies.

In some European countries efforts were made to suppress quackery by legislation—which in time proved ineffective—but no serious action of this sort was taken in the United States. The habit of self-dosing was old and well established and was a cheaper and easier procedure than going to the doctor. Physicians often protested indignantly, but were met by the usual suspicion that they desired a monopoly over prescriptions for their own profit. Today quackery is somewhat restrained by law and by confidence in medical science but such was not the case in the past century.[49]

Medical sectarianism also reached its zenith in this country by the 1850's. The major sect, homeopathy, was of German origin. Hahnemann had evolved a late eighteenth-century "system," which ascribed most forms of illness to an "internal psora" (the Itch) and promised cures on the basis of the "like cures like" formula—especially if the indicated drugs were administered in high dilutions.

Originally this system was as respectable as any other—say that of Rush—but Hahnemann survived into the era of the Paris school. French clinicians doubted his theories and viewed his remedies as useless. When some practitioners in Western Europe and America rallied to Hahnemann's support, their colleagues began to view them askance and eventually refused to deal with them. Nothing daunted, the homeopaths gradually founded their own institutions after about 1840—societies, colleges, hospitals, and pharmacies—and so a complete, unorthodox guild appeared in competition with the regular ("allopathic") profession. The first homeopathic school in the United States, subsequently termed the Hahnemann Medical College, was founded at Philadelphia in 1848; and in 1860 similar schools were established in New York and Chicago.[50]

The gradual shift in the status of homeopathy, from the dignity of a system to the heresy of a sect, may be viewed as a turning point in medical thought. Speculative short cuts were no longer to be tolerated in regular medicine. But the implications of homeopathic practice were something else again.

In a day when clinicians were condemning heroic practice, homeopaths "went them one better" by prescribing drugs so diluted that they must have been entirely innocuous. But there was one important difference here. The clinicians could only recommend that nothing be done, and such nihilism seemed too negative to most practitioners and doubtless also to their patients. Hence most of the former were still bleeding and purging in the 1840's and even in the fifties. Homeopaths, in contrast, avoided the extremes of both nihilism and heroic practice.

Like the rank-and-file regulars, Hahnemann's followers promised help, but help in the form of pleasant "water medicine" and sugar pills instead of castor oil and calomel. No wonder that homeopathy acquired some popularity. It is a plausible surmise, indeed, that the success of this sectarian guild brought more pressure on the regulars in favor of moderate practice than did all the appeals of nihilistic clinicians.

Homeopathy, with its learned background, always maintained a certain professional standing. Physicians who became unhappy about regular medicine became homeopaths or sometimes "eclectics"—the latter constituting a sect which could claim antecedents running back to Boerhaave. Less educated men, who yearned to practice but would not or could not attend regular medical schools, turned to native sects of empirical origin. Notable were the "botanics" or Thomsonians, who also revolted against calomel and used only botanic drugs. The "Dr." Thomson who founded this movement was unusual in that he patented his system, selling rights to practitioners—a type of commercialism which could not be tolerated by either regulars or homeopaths. Thomsonians also formed "friendly botanic societies" in many towns, within which families could buy in advance a right to treatments as these were necessary.[51]

Such contract practice, incidentally, was one of the few evidences in nineteenth-century America of organized concern about the costs of medical care for the masses. And even this scheme could claim little respectability. The health insurance concepts of the late 1700's survived only in the Marine Hospital system. No one seems to have advocated that such a program be applied to other groups, though a few German physicians were already thinking along this line by about 1860. Medical costs were still relatively low, of course, at a time when specialization in practice was still in the future and when all but the very poor commonly remained at home during illness. Fees for home calls were apparently as high as at present, but it was usually only the family doctor who had to be paid.

Both Thomsonians and eclectics established societies and journals, and so confronted the regulars with still other heretical guilds to combat. All the sects, along with the hygiene and "water-cure" cults had one thing in common—their condemnation of regular medicine as futile and dangerous. The regulars were not in a strong position to fight back. Their own schools, for example, were apparently deteriorating under proprietary pressures.

In addition, the regular faculties were often rent by dissensions within as well as by rivalries without. The personal quarrels between colleagues which had appeared before 1800 were multiplied thereafter as the number of schools mounted. This melancholy story is writ large across the annals of most medical colleges during the era. Daniel Drake ascribed these quarrels to envy, competition (financial as well as academic), differences in scientific opinion, and the lack of presiding authority.[52] The last point is interesting, in that it again suggests that the control of schools by their own faculties was not an unmixed blessing.

Another source of some irritation within the profession after 1850 was the unexpected intrusion of women into its ranks. This phenomenon, so startling to Victorians, had its origins in a feminist movement which was particularly active in the United States. The chief argument in favor of admitting women to the profession was that of abstract justice, but both sides in the ensuing debate appealed to Victorian sentiment as well. Advocates insisted that women should have the services of their own sex as a matter of delicacy—particularly in connection with obstetrics and gynecology. Logically, as far as obstetrics was concerned, the plea might have been one for a revived and improved midwifery; and efforts in this direction actually were made in Boston during the 1840's. But women who desired full professional rights could not be content with the status of midwives.

Most men and probably the majority of women viewed feminism with abhorrence and the thought of "female doctors" as absurd. (Because it took strong-willed persons to demand "rights" under these circumstances, it was assumed that only "long-haired men and short-haired women" would ever support the idea.) Women as such were held to be unqualified, mentally and physically, for the tasks of medicine. Their "sphere" was the home, and to take them out of it and into medical schools was condemned as both indelicate and dangerous.

Despite attitudes of this sort, a few courageous (or brazen) women persisted in their plans. Elizabeth Blackwell took the first regular M.D. at Geneva Medical College about 1850; and in the same year the Woman's Medical College was founded in Philadelphia. With the exception of Western Reserve at Cleveland and certain sectarian schools, no institutions opened their doors to medical coeducation until about 1870. The fact that sectarian colleges were relatively hospitable, however, enabled them to pose as more liberal than the regular schools on this issue.

Additional women's colleges were founded in New York and other cities during the two decades after 1850. Most physicians refused to have anything to do with their graduates and no medical societies admitted them before 1870. Thus women M.D.'s had to penetrate professional defense "in depth." It is interesting, however, that a few men always supported the "female colleges" and that the immigrant class—perhaps because they remembered midwives in the old countries—took kindly to "the doctoring ladies." Obliviously, the professional education of women was a social rather than a medical heresy—one which happened to involve medical as well as other institutions.[53]

There were further matters which embarrassed regular physicians during this era, for example, the excessive number of practitioners in their ranks. Many men who had had no formal training must still have been in practice during the forties and the growing number of schools was constantly adding to the total number licensed. An A.M.A. committee reported in 1848 that the American ratio of "physicians" to population was five times as high as in France. By 1860 there was one practitioner to every 572 persons (as compared to 1:764 in 1938). The proportion was apparently higher in rural than in urban areas—just the reverse of the present situation. Rural doctors were then more self-sufficient than they are today in an era of hospital-centered practice.[54]

Such a surplus of "medicos" weakened the profession as a whole.

It also involved recriminations between small-town and city schools and between the old medical centers and institutions in the hinterlands of the South and West. Holmes referred caustically to many "inferior schools wrongly located" and thus brought down upon himself a torrent of provincial scorn for "hifalutin Boston notions." [55]

Last but not least among the handicaps of the regular guild was the limited effectiveness of their own practice. Their leaders admitted that there was little the doctor could do against most types of illness. This seemed a weak response to the enthusiastic claims of sectarians, and no effective reply would be found until medical science began to promise utility after 1875.

On the other hand, if the regulars stuck to their heroic tradition they were condemned by the popular revolt against this which the sectarians had aroused. Thus they were damned either way. The same Dr. Arnold who was quoted above wrote during a yellow fever epidemic in 1854: "The wiseacres abused me at the corners of the streets, (I'll assure you this was literally the fact) for being old fashioned, and for killing all my patients with the Lancet and Calomel." [56]

Yet fight back the regulars did. They had the advantage of a learned tradition and conservative elements in society tended to support them. Their more candid leaders recognized the difficulties in the situation and published papers on "the declining state of the medical profession." [57] They also realized that their guild had never attained in America the status long enjoyed by law and by divinity.[58] But, closing ranks against a multitude of dangers, they rounded out the network of state and local medical societies which had already been partially established by 1820. And these societies appealed to state legislatures to protect the standing of regular medicine.

During the forties and fifties the battle seemed to go against the regulars. Such laws as were passed to limit practice to orthodox M.D.'s were unenforced in most cases. Efforts to prevent legislatures from chartering sectarian colleges or from recognizing sectarian practitioners rarely achieved more than a delaying action. In the

1840's Alabama exempted Thomsonians from penalties, Georgia licensed them by special acts, New York abandoned all restrictions except those against "gross ignorance" and malpractice, and Louisiana just gave up the enforcement of medical legislation. Some western states provided no professional regulations prior to the Civil War. By 1845 ten states had repealed their licensing laws, eight had never had any, and in only three was there any pretense of enforcement.[59]

The reaction of the legislatures, still suspicious of professional monopolies, was well illustrated by the views of a state senator at Albany who introduced a bill in 1844 to repeal licensing restrictions. He proclaimed boldly:

> A people accustomed to governing themselves, and boasting of their intelligence, are impatient of restraint. They want no protection but freedom of inquiry and freedom of action.[60]

Thus did Jacksonian Democrats proclaim their inalienable rights to life, liberty, and quackery.

The most ambitious move on the part of the regulars was the organization of the American Medical Association in 1847. Efforts to secure a national body in the 1830's had been fruitless, but in 1846 a preliminary meeting in New York laid plans for the formal organization adopted in Philadelphia the following year. Models for such a national program were already available in certain European countries, as well as in such native societies as the American Statistical Association and the American Association for the Advancement of Science.

The A.M.A. was rather loosely organized by representatives of both medical schools and societies. Its prime purpose was the reform of medical education, but it also hoped to encourage research, improve public health, and raise the level of professional ethics. Standing committees were appointed on such matters as hygiene, medical literature, and education. The A.M.A. was largely led by professors in the older schools, but was permeated nevertheless by representatives of the proprietary institutions. It was this latter situation, basically, which prevented the A.M.A. from doing much for medical education before the end of the century. The association never forgot the issues involved, however, and in time became the agent of genuine reform.

Despite all the difficulties which have been mentioned up to this point, one may well ask whether the American medical profession actually did deteriorate over the era 1820–1860. Viewed from the present standpoint, conditions were indeed scandalous at that time. But one should also look at the story from the vantage point of 1820.

True, in 1850 numerous students were mediocre persons who attended mediocre schools; but in 1820 many had had no formal education whatever. True, in 1850 rival sects competed with regulars and licensing bars were down. But in 1820 such bars as had been raised were easily surmounted. And instead of sects one then had had rival "systems" ensconced within the profession itself. The appearance of sects—at least of the more substantial ones—simply indicated popular support for "systems" which a more critical guild would no longer tolerate in its own fold. As Worthington Hooker of Yale pointed out in 1852, the rejection of these speculative programs was really a measure of progress within the regular profession.[61]

It was true, finally, that Morgan's concept of a superior guild had not been realized—despite all the M.D.'s granted—except among the graduates of a few major schools. But there were at least more of this latter type by 1860 than there had been in 1820. The mass of practitioners in 1860 were still second-class doctors but—unlike the medical men of that type in 1820—they had at least a bowing acquaintance with formal education.

The outcomes were similar, in fact, to those abroad. American professors occasionally expressed satisfaction over the fact that this country did not countenance practicing apothecaries. But British apothecaries at this time were actually raising their standards, and the goal of both British and American reformers was much the same—the production of "the safe general practitioner."[62]

Indeed, E. H. Clarke—writing in 1876—claimed only that the average American doctor was "as well equipped for practical work" as were the English apothecary and the German *Secundär Arzt*.[63] The only difference was that Europeans *labeled* their second-class guilds, whereas Americans drew no sharp lines and gave the same title to all. The latter tendency had been inherited from colonial days and continued long after 1876. To this day chiropractors are still called "doctors." Such attitudes, of course, are not limited to medical matters. American railroads, for example, have long provided distinctive travel facilities but rarely designate them as first and second class.

As far as the medical men of 1860 were concerned, the lack of open distinctions between the well-educated and the others doubtless involved both the merits and the disadvantages of equalitarianism. It probably eased the transition of able individuals from one level of attainment to another. On the other hand, the pretense that all men holding degrees were genuine physicians tended to camouflage the actual situation.

In summing up it may be held that, although professional conditions in the United States deteriorated in certain respects after 1820 —as in the lowering of premedical requirements—the general trend was one of some ultimate promise. Much of the pessimism of conscientious leaders may be ascribed to the raising of their sights rather than to actual backsliding.

Space does not permit here any real account of the guilds which supplemented the medical profession, notably those of dentists, pharmacists, opticians, and veterinarians. The first two definitely emerged in the United States during this period, and the history of their activities presents both analogies and contrasts to the story of general medicine. Just a few words may be said about dentistry and also on pharmacy by way of illustrating this generalization.

Dentistry was, in effect, the first full-time specialty in American medical practice; and the fact that it broke off from the medical profession may be ascribed in part to the latter's disinclination—

as late as 1860—to recognize specialization of any sort. During the 1830's some dentists were M.D.'s and some medical schools gave a little dental training. But in the face of wide need for dental care most medical colleges did little in this field. Hence the better educated and more ambitious dentists established schools, societies, and journals of their own after 1840 and followed this by organizing a national association even before the advent of the A.M.A.

Between 1830 and 1860 the professional history of dentistry recapitulated in many respects that of medicine during the latter half of the preceding century. In both cases there were pioneer colleges, similar efforts to standardize the licensing of both graduates and "empirics," and the same desire to grant the former a preferred status. The issue among physicians concerning the relative merits of "science" and of "practical medicine" took, among dentists, the form of debates re the relative values of "dental science" and of "mechanical dentistry." [64]

Dentists, by the very nature of their work, were always in danger of being relegated to the level of technicians. Yet by 1860 they were acquiring a better status in this country than in Europe, and they represented the first medical field in which Americans attained pre-eminence.

As mentioned in a preceding chapter, drug shops kept by pharmacists rather than by practitioners were becoming common in large towns by 1820. Urban doctors, meantime, were at last following Morgan's lead in giving up drug selling. The "apothecaries" or "druggists" had been trained simply by apprenticeship, and their leaders soon urged some formal education much as had physicians a half century earlier. In the 1820's schools of pharmacy were founded in Philadelphia and New York City. Rather isolated at first, these institutions were later joined by similar ones in Boston and in Baltimore. Local societies ("colleges") were set up, and in 1852 the American Pharmaceutical Association was established.

As in the case of medicine, the early pharmaceutical schools continued to require an apprenticeship prior to formal education. The medical schools offered no training in pharmacy, so that the nascent pharmaceutical profession had a free field in attempting to raise its own standards.

The problems were complex. They involved, first, the same contrast between "empirics" and graduates as obtained in medicine and in dentistry. In addition, pharmacists had to struggle against a popular desire for cheap remedies and were constantly tempted by the profits of the "patent medicine" trade. Physicians in this period frequently complained of the sale of low-grade or adulterated drugs and of the consequences in their practice. The states did nothing to control the situation, so attenuated was the tradition of "medical police" in this country. But, as in the cases of medicine and dentistry, the pharmaceutical guild gradually raised its sights in the large cities between 1820 and 1860.

It may be noted that the early pharmaceutical schools, like many of the medical colleges, were independent institutions with no university connections. In 1868, however, the University of Michigan introduced training in pharmacy which involved no apprenticeship. This superior program seemed to threaten the traditional colleges and the latter were therefore stimulated to organize in 1870 a Conference of the Schools of Pharmacy. It became the purpose of this body, thereafter, to set national standards in pharmaceutical education.[65]

The era 1820–1860 naturally witnessed an increase in all types of medical institutions. Many new periodicals were founded by individual professors, by faculties, and by societies, but those with the highest scientific standards continued to be the *Boston Medical Journal* and the *American Journal of the Medical Sciences*.

Institutional libraries grew slowly in contrast, and as late as 1850 an A.M.A. committee reported that the pioneer collection in the Pennsylvania Hospital was still the largest in the country. No doubt the fact that medical schools were self-supporting tended to inhibit the growth of their libraries. The schools in Philadelphia, moreover, had access to the collections in the Pennsylvania and in the College of Physicians. Similar opportunities became available in New York

City after the founding (1849) of the Academy of Medicine—an elite body somewhat similar to the Philadelphia College.[66]

Most significant was the gradual growth in the number of hospitals—chiefly in large cities. Although some of these institutions recognized in principle a responsibility in medical education and even for research, the pressures behind their founding were largely social in nature. Urban growth increased the needs of the medically indigent and prevailing humanitarianism rose to the occasion. The general trend was thus essentially a continuation of that which had appeared in New York and Philadelphia during the preceding century.

The impetus in founding hospitals came from individual laymen, from humane societies, and from groups of doctors. Funds were raised by public subscription, conducted somewhat as are community fund drives at present, and not infrequently supplementary grants were received from legislatures. The largest donations naturally came from the merchant class, but medical men, clergymen, and even farmers contributed.

Clergymen also served the hospital cause as leaders of public opinion. But by 1820 they had largely withdrawn from medical practice—though vestiges of this continued to elicit protests from physicians as late as the 1850's.[67] Hence they played no particular role in the organization or services of the new institutions.

Municipal hospitals, such as the Philadelphia General and Bellevue, were maintained by public funds and took in only charity patients; but the majority of institutions—even those which received some state aid—were privately supported and expected patients to pay what they could. Most of them, like the original Pennsylvania, were controlled by private trustees, though in the case of the Massachusetts General (1821) the state retained representation on the board.

Private control usually meant lay control, though in one or two instances—such as that of the mental hospital known as the Hartford Retreat (1823)—the state medical society named the trustees. This form of government protected the physicians from what they might view as outside interference, just as they were similarly protected in staff-owned medical schools.

John Morgan, who had unsuccessfully opposed the trustees of the Pennsylvania back in 1783, would doubtless have approved the Hartford arrangement. But that plan lessened staff responsibility to the public, and something therefore may be said for the prevailing control by lay boards. It was these bodies, for example, which forced certain hospitals to open their doors to women students after 1860—against the nearly unanimous opposition of medical staffs and societies. One wonders in passing, however, why the compromise arrangement of appointing both lay and staff members on the boards was not more often adopted.[68]

The *vox populi,* as expressed by lay trustees, was not necessarily the *vox dei*. It was the prevailing moral outlook which led some general hospitals to refuse admission to venereal cases, and there were lying-in hospitals which accepted only married women. So noted a physician as Samuel Gross criticized the Vienna lying-in hospital for its care of the "bad woman." The disinclination to help sinners, which Cotton Mather had voiced in 1724, was still maintained in the mid-nineteenth century.

The first specialized hospitals set up in the United States were those devoted to mental illness: the early precedent of the Virginia asylum founded in the 1770's has been mentioned. No other such institution was available until the Friends' Hospital was opened to mental patients of that persuasion near Philadelphia in 1813. The similarly private Hartford retreat was founded a decade later. Meantime two general hospitals—the Massachusetts (1818) and the New York (1821)—opened psychiatric branches. The Pennsylvania did not follow this example until 1841. All these were "voluntary" institutions which experienced great difficulty in meeting the costs of long-term care. A few patients could pay their way, and in certain cases some public funds were provided.

The fact that most families became medically indigent in the face of mental illness eventually led to a demand for state institutions. The way was led in this period by Kentucky, which opened a state hospital in 1824. Notable was the establishment of the Worcester State Hospital by Massachusetts in 1833. That example was favorably known to Dorothea Dix when she crusaded successfully, during the next two decades, for additional state hospitals which would provide humane care. It is of some interest that this extraordinary reformer also secured institutional improvements in the treatment of "the insane" in such distant countries as Great Britain and the Papal States.[69]

Some types of special hospitals well known in Europe, such as the "fever hospitals" of England, were not reproduced in this country. The chief types beside the mental which appeared in American cities before 1860 were maternity hospitals and those devoted to the treatment of eye and ear conditions. A lying-in hospital had been founded in New York City, for example, as early as 1798. Merged with the New York Hospital in 1801, the two institutions separated in 1827. Maternity hospitals remained rare, however. The small proportion of deliveries which were not conducted in homes could usually be cared for in special wards of the general hospitals.

During the decade from 1821 to 1830 eye and ear hospitals were established in New York, Philadelphia, and Boston; and by the fifties such institutions appeared in cities throughout the country. This trend may be ascribed in part to the technical equipment needed and in part to the fact that a nascent specialty in ophthalmology was already taking form.

One finds little evidence of private hospitals in the modern sense, save where infirmaries were attached to proprietary medical schools. But new types of sponsorship for nonprofit, general hospitals appeared in the forties and fifties, notably that of the churches. Catholic and Lutheran institutions came in, as it were, with the immigration of those decades. Whether because of these examples or for other reasons, Protestant churches of British background returned to the hospital tradition in this same period. Hence Episcopalian, Presbyterian, and Methodist institutions—as well as Jewish hospitals—appeared in the larger cities.

Most Protestant and Jewish hospitals were governed by self

perpetuating boards, much as were other voluntary institutions except that these bodies were made up of leaders in the respective denominations. Catholic hospitals were usually placed under episcopal authorities or were controlled by nursing orders. Lutheran establishments and a few Anglican also were served by nursing sisters but other Protestant groups depended on employed, secular nurses. Both men and women were employed in this connection but, lacking formal training, their status was hardly better than that of domestic servants. Most medical practice, down to about 1840, seemed to demand little more than practical experience on the part of bedside attendants.

A partial exception to this rule was to be observed in maternity care, in which field—in the absence of midwives—a few doctors displayed concern about the quality of nursing. In Philadelphia during the 1830's, for example, Dr. Joseph Warrington of the Dispensary organized a Nurse Society—composed largely of Quaker ladies—whose purpose was to provide what would now be termed obstetrical nurses. Women were recruited, given talks by Dr. Warrington, certified after some practice, and sent out to serve under supervision. Nurses were paid by the society, which in 1850 provided them with a Home.

It was also hoped to offer some general nursing for the poor, and the arrangement reminds one somewhat of the *Dames et Filles de Charité* introduced into France by St. Vincent de Paul in the seventeenth century. But, in practice, the Nurse Society received calls only in obstetrical cases. One can hardly call Dr. Warrington's program a nursing school but it was a step in that direction.

The advent of the first women's medical schools and hospitals, 1850–1860, prompted the first serious efforts to train nurses. Women, as physicians, were on trial and were anxious that their hospitals or infirmaries should be above reproach. Hence they were concerned about nursing almost from the start. In 1860 Dr. Marie Zakrzewska, upon being appointed professor of obstetrics at the New England Female [Medical] College in Boston, began training a few women there as nurses. The next year she introduced the same idea into the New England Hospital for Women and Children at Roxbury—a type of institution which was coming in at that time. There she gave formal training to thirty women over the next decade. These students gave their services to the hospital for six months in exchange for instruction—an arrangement which helped them to enroll but which, in later periods, enabled hospitals to exploit cheap service.

In 1861, meantime, the Woman's Hospital in Philadelphia opened a nursing school but secured no students until '63. The idea of a "trained nurse" was still so novel that candidates were scarce. The women's hospitals in the States, moreover, had no such prestige as was accorded Miss Nightingale's school in London in these same years. The latter possessed its own endowment, was not subject to exploitation by the hospital, and was able to set aside upper-class students who were "trained to train"; that is, to set up other schools in other hospitals. The Nightingale plan therefore spread in England and by the 1870's inspired the founding of similar schools in the United States. The early efforts of the women's hospitals in this country, in contrast, remained isolated; but they at least suggest that a few Americans were feeling their way toward a program in nursing education by the 1860's.[70]

In concluding a discussion of hospitals, one may pay tribute to their services and at the same time recognize their limitations. They existed only in the chief cities and their clientele was largely limited to the poor. Although they cared for a few middle- and upper-class patients, the vast majority of the latter were treated in their own homes. And among the poor there was doubtless some fear of these institutions, though this is difficult to document. Some patients, removed from squalid tenements, probably received better care in wards than they had known before but others must have been frightened by the alien environment in which they were suddenly confined.

There were individual doctors who were praised for their humane attitudes toward "inmates," but both scientific and social circumstances probably inhibited such attitudes. Insofar as staff members responded to the "best medicine of the day" they were inclined to see "cases" rather than human personalities in the course of their rounds. The subjective factors in illness, except perhaps in mental illness, received less attention by clinicians during the nineteenth century than in any period before or after.

Overlapping with such "objectivity" on the part of a hospital staff was, perhaps, some indifference to the poor in the wards. There was, after all, a social and educational gap in this setting between the doctor and his patient; and recent studies indicate that the qualities considered essential to a good therapeutic relationship vary "inversely with social distance between the participants."[71] The fact that this is true today does not prove that it was true in 1850, but it is a plausible surmise that social behavior has not changed much in this respect over the past century.

Such attitudes as objectivity or even indifference, insofar as they obtained in the hospitals of 1850, may be justified in some measure by their values in association with research. Dr. Redman's plea to Dr. Morgan during the preceding century—that the doctor should devote himself entirely to "doing good"—had to be overcome in some degree if there was to be any medical progress. This point therefore raises the question: To what extent did hospitals play a role in advancing medical education and science?

The answer is relatively simple. Clinical teaching, supplementing lectures, was developed in the wards of general hospitals in a few large cities, notably in Philadelphia, Boston, and New York. In the latter city Valentine Seaman even encouraged students to dress wounds—thus partially anticipating the later roles of clinical clerks and surgical dressers. But in the majority of schools, many of which had no hospitals available, bedside teaching was nonexistent.

Much the same thing may be said of the hospital role in research. The pathologic investigations of such men as James Jackson, Sr., and of William Gerhardt were made, respectively, in the general hospitals of Boston and Philadelphia. And in certain mental hospitals doctors sought to apply "the numerical method" so as to prove the success of their treatments. Though the results were misleading, these men at least tried! But in many hospitals there was no such record, nor was there any concept even in the best centers of such systematic and intensive research as was carried on in the hospitals of Paris, London, and Vienna in these years. Even James Jackson, when Pierre Louis wrote to urge that his son give four years entirely to investigating disease, replied that such full-time studies "would have been so singular, as in a measure to separate him from other men." [72]

In some degree, of course, hospitals were more sinned against than sinning. It was not their fault, for example, that most families would not give permission for autopsies. But there were physicians who—as in the case of Samuel Jackson—blamed the difficulties of research on "the paucity" and "miserable mismanagement" of hospitals. Whether the latter could have been better managed, under all the circumstances of the time, is a nice question.

In the midst of efforts to advance science and to improve institutions, how fared it with the health of the American people? Presumably better health was the ultimate goal of all medical programs. But there was in general no clear correlation between medical strivings and public well-being from 1820 to 1860. Judging by the statistical evidence, health improved slightly over the country as a whole but deteriorated in the large cities. Whether things would have been worse if it had not been for medical services is what is usually termed an academic question.

The disease picture brightened in some respects and darkened in others. While malaria spread over the Mississippi Valley, it largely disappeared in New England and in parts of the Middle Atlantic area. Tuberculosis continued to be the chief killer, though it was now in the chronic stage in which phthisis (consumption)—rather than scrofula—was the most common form. There was some evidence that consumption was becoming almost as serious in rural as in urban areas. Other respiratory infections, particularly the pneumonias, were likewise major causes of death. Typhoid and occasionally typhus continued to appear, especially in the urban setting. The so-called "children's diseases" remained endemic and, in the case of scarlet fever, became more virulent. Last but not least, the chronic and degenerative conditions were constant factors in mortality on the upper-age levels.

Among the epidemic diseases smallpox became less common than in the preceding century as a result of vaccination. (This procedure and the use of quinine against malaria were the only instances in which medical practice had any specific impact on morbidity.) Smallpox continued, nevertheless, to be a major threat until the 1860's, for the simple reason that a large proportion of the population failed to secure the protection offered by medical science. But fear of the disease declined and was replaced by the terror aroused during the cholera pandemics of the thirties and fifties. Yellow fever retreated from the northern ports after about 1825 but continued to inspire panic in southern cities throughout the century.

Epidemics of cholera and of yellow fever momentarily stimulated general concern about public health and aroused a more lasting interest among some medical leaders in the chief cities. The view that such epidemics were occasioned by filth and miasmata steadily gained ground in medical thinking, though contagionists were still vocal as late as the 1850's. In one of the national sanitary conventions of that decade, for example, more than forty pages of proceedings were devoted to the debate on the contagious or noncontagious nature of yellow fever. This debate was paralleled by similar ones abroad.

The increasing acceptance of the doctrine of local causation (miasmata) was based on more than the evidence concerning epidemic diseases. Endemic fevers also were in the picture and became obvious in large cities. It was a plausible conclusion that rising mortality was a function of congestion of population, a relationship which had been noted as early as 1793 in Philadelphia and which the English statistician Farr later expressed in a mathematical formula. It could have been argued, of course, that congestion would facilitate the spread of contagion, but further evidence at this point seemed to indicate that urban filth and overcrowding were the chief causative factors.

No doubt many observers had been vaguely aware, before 1820, that urban mortality was highest among the poor. But not until the French physician L. R. Villermé investigated the problem during the 1820's, was this fact clearly demonstrated. (Paris was, at the time, the most advanced center in relation to public hygiene as well as to medicine in general.) Villermé, through the use of statistics, showed that mortality was not only associated with congestion but that it was a function of the living conditions of a given social class within the urban environment. Mortality rates were higher and life expectancy lower within working-class districts than they were in the better neighborhoods of French cities.[73] It followed that local conditions were involved and that if one wished to lower mortality in slums it was only necessary to make them over into a semblance of the better areas. In a word, sanitary reform was indicated.

This view, and the statistical procedures on which it was based, made a marked impression on other European observers. In Great Britain, where the conditions in manufacturing towns were serious and where a general demand for social reform was in the air by the thirties, various "sanitary surveys" were undertaken. These revealed appalling slum conditions and increased the demand for sanitary reform.[74] Parliament established the office of registrar general in 1836 in order to improve the collection of vital statistics and in 1848 set up a national board of health with some power over local authorities. Meantime "health of towns" associations, in which local officials and medical men cooperated, began to work for sanitary reform in English cities.

Historians have often viewed the British sanitary movement as incidental to the general social reform of the period, but the health drive was actually a major development. "Not even the Poor Law or the Factory question," declared a recent English scholar, "go so deep into the national life."[75] The socialist leader Friedrich

Engels, observing the English scene, viewed health conditions among "the laboring class" as the chief indictment of a capitalistic society. To socialist thinkers sanitary reform within a capitalistic setting would not be enough: the entire economic order must be changed if workers were to attain the good life.[76]

One may note here, in passing, certain implications of the sanitary reform movement for the apparently distinct matter of general medical care. Until the early 1800's those hoping to improve the health of the masses had sought to extend medical services through some scheme for national health insurance. The purpose was to make practitioners accessible to the poor. Sanitary reform, on the other hand, promised to prevent disease without resort to medical services: was not an ounce of prevention worth a pound of cure? Note also that this was the very period when, in a day of "clinical nihilism," well-informed men had little faith in cures in any case.

It was probably not an accident, then, that concern about health insurance—in either national or voluntary form—declined as interest in "public health" mounted. Even socialists do not seem to have returned to health insurance concepts until after 1860. The shift in interest was symbolized by the fact that Edwin Chadwick, the English leader, began his career with the study of voluntary insurance as provided by benefit societies, but subsequently gave all his attention to sanitary reform.[77]

British reports made a deep impression on public-spirited Americans, whether physicians or laymen. A one-man sanitary survey was conducted in New York City by Dr. J. H. Griscom in 1845, and this was followed by Lemuel Shattuck's better-known report on Massachusetts in 1850. The National Institute at Washington urged a national survey and, when Congress proved indifferent, helped to pursuade the newly formed A.M.A. to examine conditions in the larger cities of the United States. The resulting reports indicated that just such poverty and disease as obtained in London, Manchester, and Glasgow also disgraced New York, Philadelphia, and Boston and that the death rates were even higher in American cities.[78]

Since all such reports were hampered by the lack of adequate data, efforts were also made to follow the British example in improving statistical services. The American Statistical Society, founded in the late thirties, worked vigorously for state legislation along that line and Massachusetts, alone among the states, provided in the forties for the collection of vital data. The A.M.A., in 1848, appointed committees to press the issue in every state, and some response was secured in eight of them between 1850 and 1860. But in most cases, individualism and plain ignorance prevented action. When a registration bill was presented in the Georgia legislature in 1849 the members "fairly hooted at the idea" and dismissed it as just another "trick of the doctors." [79]

No state health boards were established before 1870, although the Shattuck report had strongly urged such action. Sanitary reform was thus left in the hands of local authorities. Permanent boards of health had been set up in most large cities before 1820, but health administration did not take modern form until after 1860. Most boards had only advisory powers, and the actual enforcement of regulations was still loosely divided among quarantine officers, street-cleaning inspectors, sewage officials, and the like. Political corruption added to the confusion—as in New York City, where the head of the street-cleaning department had an annual appropriation of about $1 million to distribute among his party followers.[80]

Some progress was made, however, in various cities. Practically all large places possessed public water supplies and drain sewers by the 1850's, and certain cities introduced sewage systems as well. One of the most remarkable achievements was that of Savannah, where wet cultivation of rice near the city was eliminated at public expense by 1823. It was claimed that mortality was reduced by more than two-thirds as a result of this measure alone.[81]

There is no evidence that the majority of physicians took much interest in sanitary reform. Indeed, the movement was not based on any special medical knowledge and was not aimed at any particular diseases. The data employed were social and statistical in nature, and engineers and statisticians played more of a role at times than did medical men. The whole spirit in public health work, indeed, was the antithesis of the prevailing emphasis in medical science on the study of specific diseases.

A few public-spirited doctors were, nevertheless, leaders in the public health movement. Such men joined with local officials, by the 1850's, in organizing "sanitary associations" in several large cities; and this cooperation foreshadowed the combination of laymen and physicians in the great voluntary health societies of the next century.

The most striking expression of lay-medical cooperation was the organization of the national quarantine and sanitary conventions of 1857–1860. These meetings were inaugurated by Dr. Wilson Jewell of the Philadelphia health board, in imitation of an international quarantine congress held shortly before in Paris. Their proceedings mirror all the public health interests of the day, including the interminable debates between contagionists and noncontagionists. They also reflect the lack of concern with specific diseases except in the case of epidemic infections. Tuberculosis, despite its mortality, was not even recognized as a public health problem.[82]

The presence of laymen may have been responsible for some of the romantic enthusiasm which crept into the conventions and, indeed, into the whole sanitary movement. Members were convinced that they were engaged in "a crusade against a gigantic and growing evil"; [83] and Dr. Jewell hailed the first meeting "as the dawn of a new era in the domain of American science." Subsequently, as Lloyd Stevenson has shown,[84] some issues arose to divide health leaders who were primarily moral reformers from those who were primarily scientists; but in the 1850's the two groups worked together in harmony.

The national sanitary conventions planned, in 1860, to resolve themselves into a national public health association, but the Civil War intervened and this end was not realized until the seventies. Nevertheless, the conventions led the way and were a milestone in the history of the public health in this country.[85]

The final word on health conditions in the United States, during the first half of the nineteenth century, is that expressed in such vital statistics as are available. These may be summarized briefly, since their general import has already been suggested. Despite the rising crude mortality rates in large cities, the Massachusetts data showed a slight increase in general life expectancy at birth between 1790 and 1850. To be specific, the figure for males rose from 34.5 years in 1790 to 38.3 in 1850; that for females from 36.5 to 40.5 during the same interval. It may be added that such expectancy continued to increase in the same, gradual manner during the rest of the century. The figure for females, for example, rose from 40.5 in 1850 to 44.5 in 1890.[86]

These slow but definite trends are more meaningful than any death rates which could be assembled. They suggest what one would expect, namely, that gradual improvement in living conditions was a major influence, in the last analysis, in making for a similarly gradual increase in the life prospects of average individuals.

Hidden behind these crude outcomes, of course, was a balance of all those factors which benefited and all those which threatened health. Medical practice, for example, was ranged in the first of these categories when it provided vaccination and quinine, but fell in the second insofar as it was given to heroic extremes. But it will be noted, in this last connection, that the situation was definitely improving by 1860. We can now see, moreover, what was hidden to the observers of that era; namely, that science was moving—however slowly in the United States—toward the creation of a type of medicine which would eventually exert a profound influence on the health of the American people.

Notes

1. Morgan, *A Discourse upon the Institution of Medical Schools in America* (Philadelphia, 1765; reprinted Baltimore, 1947), *passim.*

2. R. H. Shryock, "The American Physician in 1846 and in 1946," *Jour. Amer. Med. Assn.,* CXXXIV (1947), 417 ff.

3. J. C. Lettsom, *Recollections of Dr. Rush* (London, 1815), pp. 12 ff.

4. Elisha Bartlett, *The Philosophy of Medical Science* (Philadelphia, 1844), p. 225. See also W. Hooker, "The Present Mental Attitude and Tendencies of the Medical Profession," *New Englander,* X (n.s., IV) (1852), 548–568.

5. Thus the crude death rate reported in New York City rose from 1 death per 46.5 persons (*ca.* 2,150 per 100,000) in 1810 to 1 in 27 (*ca.* 3,703 per 100,000) in 1859; C. F. Bolduan, "Over a Century of Health Administration in New York City"; New York City *Dept. of Health Monograph Ser.,* No. 13 (1916), 3.

6. Holmes, "Currents and Counter-Currents in Medical Science" (1860), in collected papers of same title (Cambridge, Mass., 1861), pp. 11 and 26 f.

7. Quoted in R. H. Shryock, *The National Tuberculosis Association* (New York, 1957), p. 40. See also R. and J. Dubos, *The White Plague* (Boston, 1952), introductory chaps.

8. Shryock (ed.), *Letters of Richard D. Arnold, M.D., 1808–1876* (Durham, N.C., 1929), p. 18.

9. C. D. Meigs, *Females and Their Diseases* (Philadelphia, 1848), introduction.

10. See K. M. Dallenbach, "Phrenology versus Psychoanalysis," *Amer. Jour. of Psychology,* LXVIII (December, 1955), 512–525; R. H. Shryock, "The History and Sociology of Science," Social Science Research Council *Items,* X (June, 1956), 16.

11. See, e.g., Graham, *Science of Human Health* (Boston, 1839), *passim;* Shryock, "Sylvester Graham . . . ," *Miss. Val. Hist. Rev.,* XVIII (1931), 172–

183; R. S. Fletcher, "Bread and Doctrine at Oberlin," reprint from *Ohio Archaeological and Hist. Quar.* of paper read in 1938, *passim.*

12. For the English and German backgrounds to this medical movement see, respectively, G. Newman, *Health and Social Evolution* (London, 1931), pp. 50–55, and G. Meyer, *Die Sociale Bedeutung der Medizin* (Berlin, 1900), pp. 20 ff. On the American story, J. Krout, *The Origins of Prohibition* (New York, 1925), chaps. 4 and 5.

13. R. H. Shryock, "Public Relations of the Medical Profession . . . 1600–1870," *Annals of Med. Hist.*, n.s., II (1930), 324 f.

14. Between 1800 and 1830 a number of theorists proclaimed that a particular organ or body system was responsible for most illness—a sort of compromise between a generalized and a localized pathology. Thus Henry Clutterbuck of London ascribed all fevers to conditions in the nervous system (1807)—a view which had some background in Cullen and which would be maintained by others until mid-century. In the United States, Edward Miller of New York—a former pupil of Rush—traced all fevers to the stomach in a manner reminiscent of Cotton Mather's opinions; see Samuel Miller, *Medical Works of Edward Miller . . .* (New York, 1814), p. 166. And by the 1820's Broussais of Paris was ascribing most illness to gastroenteritis.

15. On the influence of surgical views see O. Temkin, "The Role of Surgery in the Rise of Modern Medical Thought," *Bull. Med. Hist.*, XXV (1951), 248 ff.; re professional reorganization, Henry Guerlac, "Some Aspects of Science during the French Revolution," *Scientific Monthly*, LXXX (1955), 93 ff.

16. The "Paris school" receives much attention in all histories of medicine. For a specific account see, e.g., Marcel Fosseyeaux, *Paris Médicale en 1830* (Paris, 1930), *passim*. On the introduction of clinical statistics see R. H. Shryock, *Development of Modern Medicine* (New York, 1947), pp. 158–161, 165–168.

17. R. H. Shryock, "The Advent of Modern Medicine in Philadelphia, 1800–1850," *Yale Jour. Biol. and Med.*, XIII (1941), 725–731.

18. See, e.g., T. D. Mitchell, "Vindication of Benjamin Rush," MS. lecture before Phila. Med. Soc., 1822, Philadelphia College of Physicians.

19. J. Maclurg, "On Reasoning in Medicine," *Phila. Jour. Med. Sciences* (*Amer. Jour. Med. Sciences*), I (1820), 224 f.

20. See J. Eckman, "Anglo-American Hostility in American Medical Literature of the Nineteenth Century," *Bull. Med. Hist.*, IX (1941), 31 ff. British physicians had been welcomed in America in the 1700's; but when Dr. Robley

Dunglison was brought over by Jefferson in the 1820's he encountered considerable criticism because of his origins; Dunglison, "Autobiography," MS., Philadelphia College of Physicians.

21. Godman, *Contributions to Physiology and Pathologic Anatomy* (Philadelphia, 1825), p. 8.

22. *Principles of Medicine Founded on the Structure and Function of the Animal Organism* (Philadelphia, 1832), p. 10.

23. See E. Ackerknecht, "Elisha Bartlett and the Philosophy of the Paris Clinical School," *Bull. Med. Hist.*, XXIV (1950), 43 ff. Bartlett's work was the most systematic of its kind but it had been preceded by somewhat similar studies; e.g., Auber, *Traité de Philosophie Médicale* (Paris, 1839).

24. E. Goldschmid, "Contributions des États-Unis à l'anatomie pathologique au début du XIXe siècle," *Archiv. Internat. d'Histoire des Sciences* (1948), p. 479; see also E. Long, *History of Pathology* (Baltimore, 1928), p. 166.

25. J. Fulton, *Physiology* (New York, 1931), pp. 76–80; G. Rosen, *The Reception of William Beaumont's Discovery in Europe* (New York, 1942), *passim;* L. G. Stevenson, "Anatomical Reasoning in Physiological Thought," in C. McC. Brooks and P. F. Cranfield (eds.), *The Historical Development of Physiological Thought* (New York, 1959), pp. 34–37.

26. W. W. Keen, *Research and Human Welfare* (Boston, 1917), p. 18.

27. See G. Emerson, "Medical Statistics . . . Showing the Mortality in Philadelphia . . . ," *Amer. Jour. Med. Sciences,* I (1828), 116 ff.

28. L. P. Yandell, *A Memoire of . . . John E. Cooke* (Louisville, 1875), *passim.*

29. *Address* (to medical graduates), Univ. of Penna., 1840, p. 11.

30. J. S. Billings, "The History and Literature of Surgery," pp. 85 ff., in F. S. Dennis, *A System of Surgery* (Philadelphia, 1895).

31. "Surgery," in *A Century of American Medicine* (Philadelphia, 1876), pp. 133–146; J. M. Sims, *Story of My Life* (New York, 1886), pp. 226 ff.

32. The setting is recalled in such a work as E. H. Pool and F. J. McGowan, *Surgery at the New York Hospital One Hundred Years Ago* (New York, 1930), pp. 63 ff.

33. Much has been written on this "discovery." See, e.g., Victor Robinson, *Victory over Pain* (New York, 1946), *passim;* and the *Jour. of the History of Medicine,* I, No. 4 (1946), which is devoted to the introduction of anesthesia abroad.

34. See, e.g., [J. E. Dexter], *A History of Dental and Oral Science in America* (Philadelphia, 1876), pp. 10 ff. Note also the forthcoming study by R. W. McCluggage on the history of the American Dental Association.

35. See, e.g., J. Nott, "Yellow Fever Contrasted with Billious Fever: Probable Insect or Animalcular Origin," *New Orleans Med. Jour.,* IV (1848), 563 ff.; and especially Phyllis Allen (Richmond), "Etiological Theory in America Prior to the Civil War," *Jour. of the Hist. of Med.,* II (1947), 489–520.

36. See Phyllis Allen Richmond, "The Nineteenth Century American Physician as a Research Scientist," *International Record of Medicine,* CLXXI (1958), 492.

37. Jackson, *Principles of Medicine* (Philadelphia, 1832), p. 10 and pref. xvii; also his *Address to the Medical Graduates of the Univ. of Penna.* (Philadelphia, 1840), p. 15.

38. See, e.g., "The American Merchant," *Knickerbocker . . . Mag.,* XIV (1839), 10 ff., 118.

39. *Democracy in America* (1835), transl. by Henry Reeve (New York, 1904), Vol. II, pp. 518, 524 ff. Daniel Drake remarked in 1847 that Americans were more obsessed with things practical than any other people, *Strictures on . . . Medical Students* (Louisville, 1847).

40. R. H. Shryock, "American Indifference to Basic Science during the Nineteenth Century," *Archives Internationales d'Histoire des Sciences,* No. 5 (1948).

41. See R. H. Shryock, *American Medical Research: Past and Present* (New York, 1947), chaps. 1 and 2.

42. Figures on the numbers of schools and students given by contemporaries vary. For the estimate above see New York State Med. Soc., *Trans.,* I (1826), 330.

43. *Medical Education in the United States . . .* (Philadelphia, 1944), p. 430.

44. See *Amer. Jour. Med. Sciences,* n.s., I (1841), 265 f.

45. Thomas Gamble, "History of the Savannah City Government," in the *Annual Report of the Mayor,* 1900.

46. See New York State Med. Soc., *Trans.*, I (1826), 347–351.

47. W. F. Norwood, *Medical Education in the United States Before the Civil War* (Philadelphia, 1944), pp. 79, 135, 143–147.

48. R. H. Shryock (ed.), *Letters of Richard D. Arnold, M.D., 1808–1876* (Durham, N.C., 1929), pp. 82 f.

49. R. H. Shryock, "Cults and Quackery in American Medical History," Middle States Council on the Social Studies *Proceeds.*, XXXVII (1939), 19–30. See also D. L. Dykstra, "The Medical Profession and Patent and Proprietary Medicines During the Nineteenth Century," *Bull. Med. Hist.*, XXIX (1955), 401–419; and M. E. Pickard and K. C. Buley, *The Midwest Pioneer: His Ills, Cures and Doctors* (Crawfordsville, Ind., 1945), *passim.*

50. For the basic ideas of homeopathy see S. C. F. Hahnemann, *Organon der Heilkunst* (Leipzig, 1829; first ed., 1810), pp. 107 and 170 ff.

51. W. G. Smillie, "An Early Prepayment Plan for Medical Care," *Jour. of the Hist. of Med.*, VI (1951), 253–257; Alex Berman, "Neo-Thomsonianism in the United States," *ibid.*, XI (1956), 133–155. On Thomsonianism in general see S. A. Thomson, *Narrative of the Life and Medical Discoveries of . . . , Written by Himself* (Boston, 1822), *passim.*

52. Drake, *Practical Essays on Medical Education and the Medical Profession* (Cincinnati, 1832; reprinted, Baltimore, 1952), pp. 96–104.

53. See R. H. Shryock, "Women in American Medicine," *Jour. Amer. Med. Women's Assn.*, V (1950), 371–379.

54. M. Fishbein, "History of the American Medical Association," *Jour. A.M.A.*, CXXXII (Dec. 7, 1946), 852; R. H. Shryock, "The American Physician in 1846 and in 1946," *ibid.*, CXXXIV (May 31, 1947), 417 ff.

55. On professional developments in the West during this period see E. F. Horine, "Early Medicine in Kentucky and the Mississippi Valley . . . ," *Jour. of the Hist. of Med.*, III (1948), 263–278.

56. Shryock, *Arnold Letters*, p. 71.

57. See, e.g., Paul F. Eve, *Present Position of the Medical Profession in Society* (Augusta, Ga., 1849), *passim;* and the paper entitled "To What Cause Are We to Attribute the Diminished Respectability of the Medical Profession in the Estimation of the American Public?" *Med. and Surg. Reporter*, n.s., I (1858), 141–143.

58. For an interesting comparison of the licensing and respective standings of the medical and legal professions see A. Z. Reed, "Restrictions upon Professions Prior to the Civil War," *The Bar Examiner,* II (1933), 31 f.

59. See C. B. Coventry, "History of Medical Legislation in the State of New York," *N.Y. Jour. of Med.,* IV (1845), 160.

60. *Ibid.*

61. Hooker, "The Present Mental Attitude and Tendencies of the Medical Profession," *New Englander,* X (n.s. IV) (1852), 557 f.

62. See C. Newman, *The Evolution of Medical Education in the Nineteenth Century* (London, 1957), chap. 5.

63. Clarke, "Practical Medicine," in *A Century of American Medicine* (Philadelphia, 1876), p. 19.

64. See the forthcoming work by McCluggage, *The History of the American Dental Association.*

65. S. M. Colcord, "The History of American Pharmacy," *Proceeds.* Amer. Pharmaceutical Assn., XLI (1893); cited in G. Sonnedecker, "The Conference of Schools of Pharmacy—a Period of Frustration," *Amer. Jour. Phar. Education,* XVIII (1954), 389–391.

66. P. Van Ingen, *The New York Academy of Medicine: Its First Hundred Years* (New York, 1949), *passim.*

67. See, e.g., David Hosack, *Observations on the Medical Character,* "P. and S." (New York, 1826); and C. A. Bartol, *Discourse on the Death of Dr. George C. Shattuck* (Boston, 1854). A great-grandfather of the writer, a New England clergyman, collaborated on a family medical manual as late as about 1860.

68. Histories are available for some of the better-known hospitals of this period; e.g., of the Pennsylvania, and further information is supplied in Packard's *History of Medicine in the United States* (Philadelphia, 1931). But see especially L. K. Eaton, *New England Hospitals, 1790–1833* (Ann Arbor, Mich., 1957), *passim.*

69. On the psychiatry and "asylums" of this period see the essays in Gregory Zilboorg (ed.), *One Hundred Years of American Psychiatry* (New York, 1944); on Dorothea Dix, the biography by Helen Marshall, *Forgotten Samaritan* (Chapel Hill, N.C.).

70. The standard, detailed history of nursing—including the American story—is M. Adelaide Nutting and Lavinia L. Dock, *A History of Nursing* (4 vols.; New York, 1907–1912). For a briefer narrative see R. H. Shryock, *The History of Nursing: An Interpretation of the Social and Medical Factors Involved* (Philadelphia, 1959), chaps. 13 and 14.

71. Ozzie Simmons, *Social Status and Public Health,* Social Science Research Council, Pamphlet 13 (New York, 1958), p. 17.

72. L. K. Eaton, *New England Hospitals, 1790–1833,* p. 201; quoting Jackson's *Memoir of James Jackson, Jr.* (Boston, 1835).

73. Villermé, "Mémoire sur la Mortalité en France, dans la Classe Aisée et dans la Classe Indigente," *Mémoires de L'Acad. Roy. de Med.* (Paris, 1828), Vol. I, pp. 51 ff.

74. See especially the so-called Chadwick report to the Poor Law Board (London, 1842).

75. Quoted in B. L. Hutchins, *The Public Health Agitation, 1833–1848* (London, 1909), p. 58.

76. See Engels, *Die Lage der Arbeitenden Klassen in England* (1844), *passim.*

77. See R. H. Shryock, "The Relation of Medicine to Society in the 1840's," in I. Galdston (ed.), *Social Medicine: Its Derivations and Objectives* (N.Y. Acad. of Med., 1949), pp. 30–43.

78. *A.M.A. Trans.,* I (1848), 305–310.

79. Shryock, *Arnold Letters,* pp. 36–39.

80. See Stephen Smith, "The History of Public Health," in M. P. Ravenel (ed.), *A Half Century of Public Health* (New York, 1921), p. 7; J. Blake, *Historical Study of the Development of the N.Y. City Department of Health* (New York, n.d.; *ca.* 1955), pp. 6–18. The most complete history of urban health administration is W. T. Howard, *Public Health Administration . . . in Baltimore, Maryland, 1797–1920* (Washington, D.C., 1924).

81. W. Duncan, *Tabulated Mortality Record of the City of Savannah* (Savannah, 1870), p. 36.

82. See, e.g., *Proceeds.,* Third Nat. San. Convention (New York, 1859), *passim.*

83. *Ibid.*, p. 229.

84. "Science down the Drain," *Bull. Med. Hist.*, XXIX (1955), 10–25.

85. For the general relations of medicine and society throughout the first half of the nineteenth century, particularly in relation to the public health, see R. H. Shryock, "Medicine and Society in the Nineteenth Century," *Journal of World History* (UNESCO), V, 1959, pp. 122–124.

86. *Historical Statistics of the United States, 1789–1945,* Bureau of the Census (Washington, D.C., 1949), p. 45.

Index